Innovation and Global Competitiveness

In the post-liberalization period, India has slowly but steadily tried to foster innovation to improve competitive efficiency of Indian manufacturing and thus boost global competitiveness of the industrial sector. Foreign direct investment was looked upon as a major source of technology paradigm shift; in recent times, industrial firms have been investing overseas, even in countries to which they used to export, based on their technological capabilities. Firms in Indian manufacturing industries have also attempted to bring about technological upgrades through imports of design and drawings (disembodied technology) against lump sum, royalty and technical knowhow fees, and imports of capital machinery (embodied technology) where the technology is embodied in the capital good itself.

This volume comprises empirical contributions on this emerging phenomenon, on a range of issues including the role of R&D; mergers, acquisitions and technological efforts; technological determinants of competitive advantages; the role of small and medium enterprises and regional patterns; technological efforts and global operations; and the role of industrial clusters in promoting innovation and competitiveness.

This book was originally published as a special issue of *Innovation and Development*.

N. S. Siddharthan is Honorary Professor at the Madras School of Economics, India. His current research interests are technology and globalization, international economics, multinational corporations, and industrial organization.

K. Narayanan is Institute Chair Professor in the Department of Humanities and Social Sciences at the Indian Institute of Technology Bombay, Mumbai, India. His research interests span the areas of industrial economics, international business, socio-economic empowerment through ICT, environmental economics, economic impacts of climate change, and development economics.

Innovation and Global Competitiveness

Case of India's manufacturing sector

Edited by
N. S. Siddharthan and K. Narayanan

Routledge
Taylor & Francis Group

LONDON AND NEW YORK

First published 2016 by Routledge

2 Park Square, Milton Park, Abingdon, Oxfordshire OX14 4RN
711 Third Avenue, New York, NY 10017

Routledge is an imprint of the Taylor & Francis Group, an informa business

First issued in paperback 2017

British Library Cataloguing in Publication Data
A catalogue record for this book is available from the British Library

ISBN 13: 978-1-138-93775-8 (hbk)
ISBN 13: 978-1-138-30005-7 (pbk)

Typeset in Times New Roman
by RefineCatch Limited, Bungay, Suffolk

Publisher's Note
The publisher accepts responsibility for any inconsistencies that may have
arisen during the conversion of this book from journal articles to book chapters,
namely the possible inclusion of journal terminology.

Disclaimer
Every effort has been made to contact copyright holders for their permission to
reprint material in this book. The publishers would be grateful to hear from any
copyright holder who is not here acknowledged and will undertake to rectify
any errors or omissions in future editions of this book.

Contents

Citation Information

The chapters in this book were originally published in *Innovation and Development*, volume 3, issue 2 (October 2013). When citing this material, please use the original page numbering for each article, as follows:

Chapter 1
Introduction to innovation and global competitiveness: case of India's manufacturing sector
N. S. Siddharthan and K. Narayanan
Innovation and Development, volume 3, issue 2 (October 2013) pp. 145–150

Chapter 2
R&D intensity and exports: a study of Indian pharmaceutical firms
Bishwanath Goldar
Innovation and Development, volume 3, issue 2 (October 2013) pp. 151–167

Chapter 3
Mergers and acquisitions, technological efforts and exports: a study of pharmaceutical sector in India
Vidhisha Vyas, K. Narayanan and A. Ramanathan
Innovation and Development, volume 3, issue 2 (October 2013) pp. 169–186

Chapter 4
Innovation and competitiveness among the firms in the Indian automobile cluster
Rahul Z. More and Karuna Jain
Innovation and Development, volume 3, issue 2 (October 2013) pp. 187–204

Chapter 5
Influence of outward-foreign direct investment and technological efforts on exports: Indian auto component firms
Neelam Singh
Innovation and Development, volume 3, issue 2 (October 2013) pp. 205–221

Chapter 6
Technological determinants of firm-level technical efficiency in the Indian machinery industry
Pradeep Kumar Keshari
Innovation and Development, volume 3, issue 2 (October 2013) pp. 223–238

Chapter 7
Exporting by Indian small and medium enterprises: role of regional technological knowledge, agglomeration and foreign direct investment
Jaya Prakash Pradhan and Keshab Das
Innovation and Development, volume 3, issue 2 (October 2013) pp. 239–257

For any permission-related enquiries please visit:
http://www.tandfonline.com/page/help/permissions

Notes on Contributors

Keshab Das is a Professor at the Gujarat Institute of Development Research, Ahmedabad, India.

Bishwanath Goldar is a Professor at the Institute of Economic Growth, University of Delhi Enclave, India. His areas of interest include industrial economics, trade and foreign investment, and environmental economics.

Karuna Jain is Director, National Institute for Industrial Engineering (NITIE), Mumbai, India.

Pradeep Kumar Keshari is based in the Head-Zonal Training Centre (North I), IDBI Bank Limited, New Delhi, India.

Rahul Z. More is based in the SJM School of Management at the Indian Institute of Technology, Mumbai, India.

K. Narayanan is Institute Chair Professor in the Department of Humanities and Social Sciences at the Indian Institute of Technology Bombay, Mumbai, India.

Jaya Prakash Pradhan is based in the Centre for Studies in Economics and Planning at the Central University of Gujarat, Gandhinagar, India.

A. Ramanathan is a Professor of Economics at the Indian Institute of Technology Bombay, Mumbai, India.

N. S. Siddharthan is Honorary Professor at the Madras School of Economics, India.

Neelam Singh is based in the Economics Department at Lady Shri Ram College, Delhi University, India.

Vidhisha Vyas is based in IILM Institute for Business Management, Gurgaon, India.

Preface

The chapters of this book are articles that originally appeared in one of the special issues of *Innovation and Development*, an inter-disciplinary international journal from Globelics network, published by Taylor & Francis. http://www.tandf.co.uk/journals/RIAD

Innovation and Development is a relatively young journal born at a particular juncture in the discourse on development. The closing decades of the last century witnessed unprecedented changes in different spheres of economies and societies. This was induced by, among others, technological innovations led mainly by information communication technology and institutional innovations, resulting in increased integration between countries under globalization. In the emerging context of heightened competition, international competitiveness became the only means of survival. With the expanding global production networks and global innovation networks, different sectors across countries got themselves located appropriately in the global value chains. Instances of high rates growth sustained even for decades tended to suggest that achieving faster economic growth is within the reach of the developing world. Unfortunately, however, the episodes of high growth turned out to be not inclusive and sustainable. The challenge, therefore, is to accomplish development that is sustainable and inclusive.

The mandate of *Innovation and Development* has its roots in this new millennium development challenge. Since the role of innovation in development is increasingly being recognized in both the developed and the developing world, an enhancement of our understanding on the interface between innovation and development might help to find ways of addressing many of the developmental issues and making growth process inclusive and sustainable. Hence, understanding the link between innovation, capacity building and development has emerged as a critical issue of concern for academia, practitioners and policy-makers, including international organizations such as the World Bank or United Nations.

But our understanding of the links between innovation and development remains at best rudimentary, notwithstanding an unprecedented increase in studies on development and innovation on the one hand and a heightened interest in development practice on the other. While the two disciplines (development studies and innovation studies) have been growing in parallel, as they are traditionally separated with limited linkages, in recent years there has been an upsurge of interest in innovation issues in development studies. At the same time, with an increasing engagement of civil society organizations in developmental issues, innovative development practices are becoming more visible and their impact felt more than ever before.

By adopting a broader approach to innovation (to include technological, institutional, organizational and others) the journal and this book series aims to provide a forum for discussion of various issues pertaining to innovation, development and their interaction, both in the developed and developing world, for achieving sustainable and inclusive growth.

It is matter of great satisfaction that *Innovation and Development* has been able to lay the strong foundations for integrating innovation studies and development studies through the high quality articles contributed by scholars across the world. These articles dealt with issues pertaining to diverse contexts ranging from primary agriculture to high-end services, and from low technology sectors to high technology sectors operating in both the developing and developed world. In tune with the Globelics research agenda, *Innovation and Development* has also been promoting research and discourse on innovation at the national, regional, sectoral and societal level to facilitate building up systems for learning, innovation and competence building. A unique feature of *Innovation and Development* is its supplementary sections that publish PhD abstracts, web resources for research and innovations in practice.

The editorial board of *Innovation and Development* also takes pride in highlighting the significant contribution of this journal during the last five years of its existence through its special issues that focused on subjects of much relevance for theory and policy. The special issues brought out by the journal dealt with issues that include:

a) Sustainability–oriented innovation systems in China and India, guest editor Tilman Altenburg;
b) Capability building and global innovation networks, guest editors Glenda Kruss and Michael Gastrow;
c) Innovation and global competitiveness: case of India's manufacturing sector, guest editors N. S. Siddharthan and K. Narayanan;
d) Innovation for inclusive development, guest editor Fernando Santiago;
e) New models of inclusive innovation for development, guest editors Richard Heeks, Christopher Foster and Yanuar Nugroho.

We place on record our appreciation for all our guest editors for joining hands with us in our endeavor to take forward the agenda of *Innovation and Development*. We also take this occasion to acknowledge the liberal support that we received from the Editorial Advisory Board and the Scientific Committee. Our special appreciation goes to Taylor & Francis for bringing out this book series from the special issues of *Innovation and Development* and Emily Ross for taking this project to its local conclusion.

It is our hope that this book series will be useful to the academia at large, innovation scholars in particular and the policy-makers concerned.

K. J. Joseph (Editor in Chief),
Cristina Chaminade, Susan Cozzens, Gabriela Dutrénit,
Mammo Muchie, Judith Sutz and Tim Turpin
Editors, *Innovation and Development*

Introduction to innovation and global competitiveness: case of India's manufacturing sector

N. S. Siddharthan[a] and K. Narayanan[b]

[a]Madras School of Economics, Chennai, India; [b]Department of Humanities and Social Sciences, Indian Institute of Technology Bombay, Mumbai, India

1. Introduction

In the post-liberalization period, India has slowly but steadily tried to foster innovation to boost global competitiveness of the industrial sector. Since innovation in Indian industries for a long time has been supported by adaptation, assimilation and incremental changes on technology transferred from overseas, reforms smoothened the progress of the inflow of foreign direct investment (FDI). Several efforts were made to facilitate technology paradigm and technology trajectory shifts, in order to improve competitive efficiency of Indian manufacturing so that they could become globally competitive. FDI was looked upon as a major source of technology paradigm shift for Indian manufacturing, especially since the research and development (R&D) intensity of majority of the firms in the manufacturing industry has been very low (less than 1%) for long period of time. Industries where R&D intensity has been higher than the national average have looked for opportunities to world markets and earned the crucial foreign exchange (Kumar 2002). Firms in Indian manufacturing industries have also attempted to bring about technological upgradation through imports of design and drawings (disembodied technology) against lump sum, royalty and technical knowhow fees, and imports of capital machinery (embodied technology), where the technology is embodied in the capital good itself. The in-house R&D efforts were often directed to adapt the imported technology to suit the local resource and market conditions.

The role played by innovation in determining global competitiveness of Indian industries has been well researched (Kumar and Siddharthan 1994; Siddharthan and Nollen 2004). Most of them report a strong positive role for technological efforts (representing innovation)] in decision to export as well as boosting export intensity (proxy for global competitiveness, Bhat and Narayanan 2009). One of the major conclusions that emerges from the literature is that the impact of FDI on export performance of industries will vary not only with respect to the conditions specific to the host economy but also according to the types of industries that FDI enter (Bhaduri and Ray 2004). Studies of the Indian economy have found that majority of the FDI in India may not have entered the export-oriented industries and therefore could have little impact on the exports of India (Aggarwal 2002). During initial stages of liberalization, Indian firms depended mainly on technology spillovers for survival (Kathuria 2002). However, in recent times, some of the Indian firms have increased their productivity, some times higher than that of developed-country MNEs. Furthermore, industrial firms from India have been investing overseas, even in countries to which they were exporting until then, based on their technological capabilities. Empirical work on this emerging phenomenon has been scarce. This special issue of *Innovation and Development* intends to fill this gap.

Technologically active firms have created a niche market for themselves with cost- and/or product-specific advantages. Some of these firms are based on industries which have large FDI presence in India and have faced severe competition in the domestic market. The emergence of these firms in the global market could be explained by their own technological search efforts and/or spillover effects. The R&D carried out by the firms in collaboration with multinationals may help maximize exports. The increasing trend in mergers and acquisitions (M&A) activities could also have serious implications for global competitiveness of Indian industries. Further, there could be industry, firm as well as local specific advantage for firms to emerge globally competitive in a more liberal world trade regime. These factors motivated us to invite papers in the theme of innovation and global competitiveness in the Indian industries context.

2. Focus

The set of six papers published in this special issue were originally presented at the Seventh Annual Conference of the Forum for Global Knowledge Sharing (Knowledge Forum http:// fgks.in), held in Pune, November 2012. The six papers deal with several issues relating to this theme. The issues relate to

- the role of R&D;
- mergers, acquisitions and technological efforts;
- technological determinants of competitive advantages;
- the role of small and medium enterprises and regional patterns;
- technological efforts and global operations;
- the role of industrial clusters in promoting innovation and competitiveness.

The papers included in this issue cover pharmaceuticals (two papers), automobile sector (two papers), industrial machinery (one paper), and regional innovation systems and small and medium firms.

While discussing global competitiveness of Indian firms, most scholars mainly refer to the Information Technology (IT) sector. In our view, the Indian pharmaceutical sector is equally competitive and export intensive. Firms from this industry have also been investing in other countries. This sector, unlike the IT sector, is under-researched and its innovative nature is not fully recognized. This special issue of *Innovation and Development* will bridge this gap. Likewise, India is emerging as an important location for automobiles industry. In this industry, the Indian firms have emerged as multinationals and have been investing and establishing manufacturing facilities in other countries. After India launched liberalization measures in the early 1990s, the Indian machine-making industry suffered a severe setback. However, soon several firms recovered and started holding their own despite stiff global competition. Appropriately this special issue cover this feature as well. Regional innovation systems and regional pattern of exports within a country is also a neglected area. One of the papers discusses this important aspect from the point of view of small and medium enterprises (SMEs). Accordingly the special issue focuses on under-researched Indian manufacturing sectors that have emerged globally competitive.

3. Liberalized regime and the Indian high technology industries

When India liberalized its trade and investment regime during early 1990s and joined the World Trade Organisation (WTO) in mid-1990s, it reduced import tariffs radically and abolished most of the quantitative restrictions on imports. Before the WTO regime came into existence, India did not grant product patents for pharmaceutical products. It granted only process patents and that too for a limited period. Under the WTO regime, India has to grant product patents for 20 years from the date of filing. Furthermore, copyrights are now protected for 50 years, and they cover several items like software, databases, recordings, performances and broadcasts (20 years). Trademarks and service marks are protected for seven years and are renewable indefinitely. Moreover, compulsory licensing and linking of foreign and domestic trademarks are prohibited. Furthermore, India could not continue with the policy of imposing domestic procurement requirements on multinational enterprises (MNEs). Several scholars felt that the policy changes introduced to fulfil WTO requirements would harm Indian industry, in particular, pharmaceuticals, automobiles and industrial machinery. It could also adversely affect the small and medium firms (SMEs).

During initial stages, liberalization did adversely affect some of the firms in these sectors. However, soon some of the firms recovered and succeeded at a global scale. There were gainers and losers due to liberalization. On the whole on hindsight, it is clear that these industries benefited by liberalization. In the case of the Indian pharmaceutical industry, critics of WTO regime painted a grim picture and vehemently argued against India agreeing to the new intellectual property protection regime. However, the data presented in this issue show a rapid growth of the industry after 1995. Thus during 1980–1995, the pharmaceutical industry grew at the rate of 6–7% per annum. Its growth rate accelerated to 13% per annum during the post-WTO regime of 2005–2011. In addition, the export intensity (exports to sales) of this industry increased from 18% during 1996 to 41% during 2010. The leading firms exported more than 50% of the output. Post-WTO regime M&A have assumed importance globally. In the Indian manufacturing industry, a maximum number of M&A have taken place in the pharmaceutical sector. Firms have been adopting corporate strategies like M&A to acquire technological and export capabilities.

In this context, the following questions assume importance:

(1) What are the causes of the success of the Indian pharmaceutical industry in the post-WTO phase?
(2) What was the role of R&D and productivity in the success of the sector?
(3) What role technological strategies play in explaining inter-firm performance?
(4) How did the Indian pharmaceutical firms developed to become MNEs?
(5) What role does M&A play in the acquisition of technology and in promoting exports?

These are some of the issues discussed in this special issue.

India also emerges as an important producer and consumer of automobiles. As the papers included in this special issue show, currently India is the second largest market for two wheelers, ninth for cars and eighth for commercial vehicles. Most of the Indian demand is met by domestic production. There are very few imports of vehicles. The growth rate of the export of Indian vehicles has also been impressive. It has been more than 20% per annum during the last decade. Like the pharmaceutical firms, Indian automobile firms have also been investing abroad. There have also been many M&A.

The automobile components sector could be divided into three groups: original equipment manufacturing (OEM) firms and first-tier suppliers and second-tire suppliers. The determinants of exports of the three groups of firms could be different and one uniform policy might not have the same effect on the three groups. There are three main auto-clusters in India. They are located in the National Capital Region; Chennai – Bangalore belt; and the Pune cluster. Studies have shown that firms located in the clusters perform better in terms of profit margins and productivities compared to firms that operate outside these clusters (Okada and Siddharthan 2008). The papers included here will discuss the following issues:

- The role of auto-clusters in promoting knowledge sharing.
- Auto-clusters and technology spillovers.
- Spillovers due to labour mobility and interaction among workers.
- Differential export behaviour of the three groups of firms, namely original equipment manu facturers and first- and second-tier suppliers.
- FDI outflows and exports – are they substitutes or complementary?

The Indian machinery industry was developed mainly in the strict import substitution regime and with huge public investments. After liberalization imports were freely allowed and the import tariffs drastically reduced. Many MNEs also established units in India. Under these conditions domestic firms could survive only if they are technically efficient and operate in the technology frontier (Ray 2006). The study included in this special issue show that out of the top five firms that are close to the technology frontier three were domestic firms. This is welcome news from the point of view of Indian firms. This leads to the analysis of the determinants of technical efficiency of firms. The paper included in this issue identifies the main determinants.

Another important issue relates to the globalization of SMEs. These enterprises play a prominent role in employment generation, value addition and exports. In this context, it is important to find out whether regional differences in accumulated technological knowledge, FDI inflows and industrial agglomeration influence export activities of SMEs. In other words, whether regional factors play a notable role in SME globalization? Studies on the impact of local resource base in terms of stock of knowledge and information in a given region has been scarce. The paper included in this issue fills this gap in the literature. In addition, there are some emerging SMEs that are 'global born' in the sense they were started with the purpose of serving the global market. These emerging features will also be studied in the paper.

4.   Guided Tour of Papers

The first two papers of the special issue analyse the export behaviour of the Indian pharmaceutical industry. The first paper by Goldar concentrates on the impact of R&D intensity and productivity advantages on export intensities of firms. The second paper by Vidhisha, Narayanan and Rama-nathan emphasizes the role of M&A and in particular the acquisition of foreign firms by Indian enterprises in promoting exports. The next two papers (papers 3 and 4) deal with the automobile sector in India. The paper by More and Jain focuses on industrial cluster and agglomeration advantages in influencing the competitive advantages of firms operating in the cluster. The paper mainly deals with the Pune automobile cluster. It uses innovation systems and global value chain perspectives to develop a framework for evaluating innovation performance and maintaining competitiveness of firms. The paper by Neelam Singh highlights the differential export behaviour of automobile firms belonging to different categories of exports, namely original equipment manufacturers and first-tier and second-tier exporters. In addition, it also explores the role of outward FDI (OFDI) of Indian firms in promoting exports. In this context, the paper extends the 'substitutability versus complementarity' hypothesis. The paper by Kesari estimates the technical efficiency of the machinery manufacturing firms and analyses their main determinants. The main argument being inefficient firms will not be able to withstand global competition, and hence, it is important to identify the determinants of technical efficiency. The last paper by Pradhan and Das investigates the importance of agglomeration and FDI on the performance of SMEs. While doing so they also bring in the role of networking and R&D facilities available in the agglomeration and access to information.

The first paper by Goldar links the R&D efforts of firms to productivity in explaining exports. He argues that a more productive firm is more likely to self-select itself into the export market.

Furthermore, the impact of R&D on exports would depend on the level of productivity already reached by the firm. The closer the firm is to the technology frontier, the greater will be the impact its R&D efforts will have on its exports. In his econometric analysis, he uses data for 319 pharmaceutical firms for a 12-year (1999–2011) period. After experimenting with several models he selects the tobit random effect model as the preferred one. For explaining entry into the export market, the paper prefers Cox proportional hazards model. While confirming the hypothesis on R&D and productivity link, his results further show that Indian pharmaceutical firms have been the main exporters and not the MNEs.

The next paper by Vidhisha, Narayanan and Ramanathan analyses the competitive advantages arising out of M&A. They suggest that industries with more M&A deals have greater penetration in international markets. Indian pharmaceutical sector leads in M&A. In this sector, 39% of the acquisitions are in the form of cross-border deals. Export intensity of M&A firms are nearly double to that of other firms. Furthermore, they enjoy higher R&D and advertisement intensities and also import more materials and embodied technology. This paper also found MNEs exporting less compared to other Indian firms. In the pharmaceutical sector, the developed countries have erected several non-tariff barriers to trade. The firm needs to register in the host country before importing drugs and the drugs themselves need to register and pass the required tests. Under these conditions, entry into the host market becomes easier if a firm acquires a firm that is already registered in the host market and sells its products through the acquired host country firm. This could be one of the reasons for the predominance of acquisition of foreign firms by Indian firms.

The paper by More and Jain presents a study of the Pune automobile cluster. The major technological issues in the automobile industry are fuel efficiency, competency of internal combustion engine, weight of the vehicles, emission norms and safety features. The paper argues that there are advantages in locating the unit in a cluster. In particular, the SMEs will benefit by being part of the technology cluster. The Pune cluster in addition to assembling vehicles produces clutch, gear, brake, engine and electrical components. Many of them are produced by SMEs. In addition, an Auto Cluster Project was set up to support SMEs in design, calibration, environment and component testing facilities. Furthermore, global OEMs have established their R&D centres in Pune. Given this environment a study of Pune cluster assumes importance. The study collects evidence from 108 auto component firms located in the cluster. The study finds both external sources of innovation and knowledge spillover externalities had influenced building innovation capabilities of firms in the cluster.

Neelam Singh's paper highlights the role of OFDI in influencing export competitiveness of auto component units in India. The paper finds a significant influence of OFDI on exports. However, an increase in OFDI beyond a certain level could harm exports. In addition, technical collaborations and R&D also promoted exports. Moreover, export behaviour differed among the three groups of firm studies, namely OEMs and first- and second-tier suppliers.

In the current WTO regime where it is difficult to erect trade barriers, firms cannot compete unless they are efficient and operate at the frontier of technical efficiency. The paper by Kesari analyses the determinants of technical efficiency of the firms belonging to the Indian machinery industry. The research is based on a sample of 178 firms covering the period 2000–2007. To compute firm- and year-specific technical efficiencies, the study estimates a stochastic frontier production function. To analyse the determinants of technical efficiency, it estimates a random effect panel data model with tobit specifications. The study shows that Indian firms improved their efficiency and competitiveness through networking and strategic alliances involving import of disembodied technology and greater use of imported inputs. In addition, in-house R&D expenditures and expenditures to promote product differentiation advantages also enhanced the technical efficiency of firms.

The sixth and last paper by Pradhan and Das emphasizes the role of regional technological knowledge, agglomeration and FDI in improving the global competitiveness of SMEs. They network with regional R&D facilities and also with other units in the region to have better access to information about overseas markets. The study shows that SMEs enjoy spillover of technology and ideas from the stock of knowledge available in the region. Thus, regions with strong agglomeration economies benefit SMEs through knowledge spillovers relating to consumers, productive resources and infrastructure. In addition, some of the SMEs are 'born global' firms and also tend to locate in regions with higher knowledge base.

References

Aggarwal, Aradhna. 2002. "Liberalisation, Multinational Enterprises and Export Performance: Evidence from Indian Manufacturing." *Journal of Development Studies* 38 (3): 119–137.

Bhaduri, S., and A. Ray. 2004. "Exporting through Technological Capability: Econometric Evidence from India's Pharmaceutical and Electrical/Electronics Firms." *Oxford Development Studies* 32 (1): 87–100.

Bhat, Savita, and K. Narayanan. 2009. "Technological Efforts, Firm Size and Exports in the Basic Chemical Industry in India." *Oxford Development Studies* 37 (2): 145–169.

Kathuria, Vinish. 2002. "Liberalisation, FDI and Productivity Spillovers – An Analysis of Indian Manufacturing Firms." *Oxford Economic Papers* 54 (4): 688–718.

Kumar, Nagesh. 2002. *Globalisation and the Quality of Foreign Direct Investment*. New Delhi: Oxford University Press, p. 274.

Kumar, N., and N. S. Siddharthan. 1994. "Technology, Firm Size and Export Behaviour in Developing Countries: The Case of Indian Enterprises." *The Journal of Development Studies* 31 (2): 289–309.

Okada, Aya, and N. S. Siddharthan. 2008. "Automobile Clusters in India: Evidence from Chennai and the National Capital Region." In *The Flowchart Approach to Industrial Cluster Policy*, edited by Akifumi Kuchiki and Masatsugu Tsuji, chapter 5, 109–144. London: Palgrave-Macmillan.

Ray, S. 2006. "The Changing Role of Technological Factors in Explaining Efficiency in Indian Firms." *Journal of Developing Areas* 40 (1): 127–140.

Siddharthan, N. S., and S. Nollen. 2004. "MNE Affiliation, Firm Size and Exports Revisited: A Study of Information Technology Firms in India." *The Journal of Development Studies* 40 (6): 146–168.

R&D intensity and exports: a study of Indian pharmaceutical firms

Bishwanath Goldar[a,b]

[a]Institute of Economic Growth, University Enclave, University of Delhi (North Campus), Delhi, India; [b]Centre for International Trade and Development, School of International Studies, Jawaharlal Nehru University, New Delhi, India

The export intensity of Indian pharmaceutical firms has increased substantially in the period after 1995 when the new, more restrictive patent regime was introduced in India. The hike in export intensity has been accompanied by an increase in R&D intensity of Indian pharmaceutical firms. The results of the econometric analysis presented in the paper indicate that increased R&D efforts of Indian pharmaceutical firms were responsible in a major way for the observed increase in export intensity. The econometric results suggest that the impact of R&D intensity on exports depends on the level of productivity already reached by the firms.

1. New patent regime, growth, R&D and exports

Prior to 1970, the Indian pharmaceuticals industry was relatively small in terms of production capacity. At the time of India's Independence in 1947, India's pharmaceuticals market was dominated by multinational companies (MNCs) which controlled between 80% and 90% of the market primarily through imports (Greene 2007). The scene changed radically with the Patent Act of 1970. Product specific patents were disregarded in favour of manufacturing process patents, which allowed Indian companies to reverse engineer or copy foreign patented drugs without paying a licensing fee. This policy initiative created a favourable environment for the domestic industry to grow and acquire technical competence. At the same time, domestic drug prices were set at very low levels under the provision of Drug Price Control Orders of 1970 and 1979. Simultaneously high import tariffs were imposed. The changed policy regime helped the domestic industry to grow rapidly. The market share of MNCs declined from 68% in 1970 to only 23% in 2004 (Chaudhuri 2005, 18, Table 2.2). The value of total production of bulk drugs and formulations at current prices rose from Rs. 4900 million in 1974–1975 to Rs. 14,400 million in 1980–1981 and further to Rs. 354,710 million in 2003–2004 due to the entry of many domestic firms along with a massive increase in the production by the older firms (Chaudhuri 2005, 40).

During the period 1970–1971 to 1979–1980, the growth rates in the value of production of bulk drugs and formulations at constant prices were about 14% and 17% per annum, respectively (Jha 2007). In the subsequent period 1980–1981 to 1994–1995, the growth rates were in the range of 6–7% per annum (Jha 2007). *Annual Survey of Industries* (Central Statistical Office, Government of India) data for the period of 1970–1971 to 1994–1995 reveal that the average growth rate in value of output of the Indian pharmaceuticals industry at constant prices was about 11% per annum in this period.

From 1995 began the process of establishing a new patent regime in India. Also, the price controls were substantially relaxed. At one stage, there were serious concerns regarding the adverse effect that the new patent regime might have on the Indian pharmaceuticals industry. However, there is now a wide recognition that the Indian pharmaceuticals industry has adopted strategies to meet the challenges of the new patent regime and has been successful at that. India has emerged a major supplier of cheap and quality supplier of generics in the regulated markets. The level of R&D activity in the Indian pharmaceutical firms has considerably increased and this has shown up in the number of applications made for patents for pharmaceutical products in India and abroad. There are other dimensions of the improvement in performance that has taken place. The Indian pharmaceutical firms have been acquiring manufacturing facilities abroad. The pharmaceutical firms have entered into various types of alliances with foreign firms. Some firms are engaged in contract manufacturing, some others are involved in contract research and product development, and in clinical trials.[1]

Despite the drastic change in the patent regime, making it a much stricter regime than before, the growth of output of the domestic pharmaceutical firms continued beyond 1995. Between 1995–1996 and 2004–2005, the average rate of growth of deflated sales of Indian pharmaceutical firms[2] was about 4%. In the subsequent period beginning 2005, when the new patent regime became fully effective, the growth rate significantly accelerated. The growth rate in deflated sales of pharmaceutical firms in the period 2005–2006 to 2010–2011 was high at about 13% per annum.

As mentioned above, in the new patent regime, there has been a substantial increase in the R&D efforts of domestic pharmaceutical firms. The research activities have certainly increased and large firms have started undertaking R&D after 1995 on a much larger scale not only for developing non-infringing processes and new formulations of existing and new drugs but also to develop new molecules. The ratio of R&D expenditure to sales has increased from about 2% in 1996–1997 to about 6% in 2008–2009 (Goldar and Gupta 2010). This hike in R&D efforts has led to increases in number of patent applications and patents granted. The number of patent applications made in India in the area of drugs and medicines increased from 211 in 1990–1991 to 2211 in 2005–2006 (Goldar and Gupta 2010). The increase in the number of patents granted was from 87 in 1990–1991 to 457 in 2005–2006 (Goldar and Gupta 2010). Similarly, there has been an increase in the number of patent applications in the area of pharmaceuticals filed by the pharmaceutical firms in India and the Council of Scientific and Industrial Research (CSIR) with the US Patent and Trademark Office. It increased from 13 in 1996 to 130 in 2008 (Goldar and Gupta 2010). Also, there has been an increase in global patent filing by leading Indian pharmaceutical firms, from 33 in 1999 to 492 in 2005 (Dhar and Gopakumar 2006, 45).

Another interesting development since 1995 is the marked increase in the export intensity of pharmaceutical companies. Taking together all corporate sector pharmaceutical firms, the ratio of exports to sales increased from about 18% in 1996–1997 to about 39% in 2008–2009 (Goldar and Gupta 2010). To take up some specific cases, the export intensity of Cipla Ltd. increased from about 10% in 1995 to about 42% in 2004, and that of Lupin Ltd increased from 0.2% in 1997 to about 47% in 2004 (Dhar and Gopakumar 2006, 34).

A recent major development in the Indian pharmaceuticals industry is the acquisition of leading Indian firms by MNCs. Some of the acquisitions that have taken place in recent years include: Matrix lab acquired by Mylan Inc., Dabur Pharma acquired by Fresenuis Kabi, Ranbaxy acquired by Daiichi Sankyo, Santha Biotech acquired by Sanofi Aventis, Orchid Chemicals acquired by Hospira and Piramal Healthcare's generic medicine unit acquired by US-based

Abbott Laboratories. With these acquisitions, the market share of multinational firms has substantially increased (by about 10 percentage points) between 2003 and 2010. The market domination of the MNCs had eroded after 1970 because of the change in patent policy along with other policy changes introduced. It seems that the foreign drug-makers are poised to regain to some extent their position in the Indian market.[3]

2. Study objective, hypotheses and models

The main objective of this study is to examine the relationship between R&D activities in Indian pharmaceutical firms and their export performance. Since R&D is expected to enhance the competitiveness of firms, and both R&D intensity and export intensity have increased significantly in the Indian pharmaceuticals industry after 1995, it would be reasonable to hypothesize that increased R&D efforts made by Indian pharmaceutical firms have contributed in a major way to improvement in their export competitiveness which has led to increased exports.[4] This hypothesis is put to test by applying econometric models.

Several earlier studies on the Indian pharmaceuticals industry have come up with empirical evidence that suggests a positive relationship between technology and export performance among Indian pharmaceuticals firms. For instance, based on her econometric analysis, Aggarwal (2004) found R&D to be a major determinant of exports among Indian pharmaceutical firms. Similarly, a significant positive correlation between change in R&D and change in exports (both normalized by sales) among Indian pharmaceutical firms has been found in the study of Goldar and Gupta (2010). Chadha (2009) studied the product cycle and neo-technology theories of trade in the context of exports of generic pharmaceuticals from India. The study covered 131 pharmaceutical firms for the period of 1989–2004. An econometric model was estimated explaining inter-firm and inter-temporal variations in exports. The results showed that technology proxied by the acquisition of foreign patents has a favourable effect on exports.

The novelty of this paper is that it brings into analysis the issue of firm heterogeneity which causes firms to self-select themselves into the export market. A substantial body of the literature has emerged on the link between firm heterogeneity and exports (see Bernard et al. 2003; Melitz 2003; Melitz and Ottaviano 2008; and a literature survey paper by Greenaway and Kneller 2007). The main point emerging from this literature is that firms differ in productivity, and a more productive firm is more likely to self-select itself into the export market.[5]

Given that the productivity level has an influence on the propensity of a firm to enter the export market, it may be hypothesized that the impact of R&D intensity on the export performance of a firm will depend on the firm's level of productivity. If the firm is close to the technology frontier as reflected in its relatively high level of productivity, R&D would have a greater impact on its export performance as compared to a firm that is much below the technology frontier and thus has a low level of productivity. This is the second hypothesis put to empirical test in this paper is respect of pharmaceutical firms in India.

Two models are used for the econometric analysis. In the first model, export intensity is taken as the dependent variable and R&D intensity, separately and in interaction with productivity, is taken an explanatory variable. Certain other characteristics of the firms are included among the explanatory variables. Thus, the model may be written as

$$XI = f(RD, RD^*TE, Z), \tag{1}$$

where XI denotes export intensity, RD denotes R&D intensity, TE denotes technical efficiency (closeness to technology frontier or the level of productivity vis-à-vis other firms) and Z is a vector of other explanatory variables, representing firm characteristics. The effect of RD on XI depends on the coefficient of RD and that of the interaction term involving RD and TE (which is denoted by RD*TE). It is hypothesized that a higher level of technical efficiency (i.e. the firm is closer to the technology frontier) will raise the effect of RD on XI. Thus, the coefficient of the interaction term of RD and TE is expected to be positive.

The equation described above has first been estimated by the ordinary least-squares (OLS) method after introducing year dummies to allow the intercept to vary over time. The equation has then been estimated by the Tobit model with year dummies. Since export intensity is zero in a significant proportion of observations, the Tobit model has an advantage over the simple regression model estimated by the OLS method. This has been followed by the estimation of the random-effects Tobit model, which has the advantage that the influence of firm-specific factors on export performance gets incorporated into the model, which is missing in the simple Tobit and OLS models. In this case, the time-invariant variables have been dropped from the equation, since the influences of these factors are picked up by the firm effects.

The three specifications of the model mentioned above, i.e. the OLS, simple Tobit and random-effects Tobit, may be written as follows:

OLS

$$XI_{it} = \alpha + \delta_t + \beta_1 RD_{it} + \beta_2(RD_{it}{}^*TE_{it}) + \sum \gamma^k Z_{it}^k + \varepsilon_{it}, \qquad (2)$$

Tobit

$$XI_{it}^* = \alpha + \delta_t + \beta_1 RD_{it} + \beta_2(RD_{it}{}^*TE_{it}) + \sum \gamma^k Z_{it}^k + \varepsilon_{it}, \qquad (3)$$

$$XI_{it} = 0 \quad \text{if} \quad XI_{it}^* \leq 0 \quad \text{and} \quad XI_{it} = XI_{it}^* \quad \text{if} \quad XI_{it}^* > 0.$$

Tobit with random effects

$$XI_{it}^* = \alpha + \delta_t + \beta_1 RD_{it} + \beta_2(RD_{it}{}^*TE_{it}) + \sum \gamma^k Z_{it}^k + u_i + \varepsilon_{it}, \qquad (4)$$

$$XI_{it} = 0 \quad \text{if} \quad XI_{it}^* \leq 0 \quad \text{and} \quad XI_{it} = XI_{it}^* \quad \text{if} \quad XI_{it}^* > 0.$$

In the equations given above, XI denotes export intensity, RD denotes R&D intensity and TE denotes technical efficiency. The subscripts i and t are for firms and years, respectively. Z is a vector of other explanatory variables, representing firm characteristics, and γ is the corresponding vector of parameters. The term δ_t represents the year effects. The random error term is denoted by ε_{it}, which is assumed to be independent and identically distributed. The term u_i in Equation (4) is the unobserved individual (or firm) effects and thus measures heterogeneity among firms. The term ε_{it} is assumed to have a normal distribution with mean zero and variance σ_ε^2. The term u_i is assumed to follow a normal distribution with mean zero and variance σ_u^2. The terms ε_{it} and u_i are assumed to be independent. In Equations (3) and (4), XI* is a latent variable which is not observed. What is observed is XI (export intensity). It is equal to XI* if XI* is positive, and it is equal to zero, if XI* is less than or equal to zero.

Estimation of the Tobit model and the random-effects Tobit model is done by the maximum likelihood method. Certain issues of econometric estimation of these two models are briefly discussed in the appendix.

The second model used for the analysis is directed at explaining firm entry into the export market. For this purpose, the Cox proportional hazard model has been applied. The Cox proportional hazards model may be written as

$$h(t|x_j) = h_0(t) \cdot \exp(\beta' x_j). \tag{5}$$

In this equation, $h_0(t)$ is the baseline hazard function, which is not estimated. It is assumed that the covariates x_j, where j is the subscript for firm j, shift the baseline hazard function. The covariates for this model have been taken to be the same as in the model in Equation (1). These include R&D intensity, technical efficiency and other firm characteristics. The parameters β are estimated by the maximum likelihood method (see appendix for some discussion on methodology). It should be pointed out here that survival is interpreted as the time for which the firm has not entered the export market. Failure is interpreted as entry into the export market. To separate out the marginal exporters from significant exporters, a cut-off level of 1% is used. In other words, only if the exports to sales ratio of a firm exceed 1%, the firm is considered to have entered the export market.

A brief discussion of studies in which the Cox proportional hazard model has been applied to analyse the survival of industrial firms and the duration of trade would be in order here. In a number of studies, the Cox proportional hazard model has been used for analysing the exit of firms from the market. To give some examples here, Esteve-Perez, Sanchis Llopis, and Sanchis Llopis (2004) have studied the survival of Spanish manufacturing firms using the Cox proportional hazard model. They find that exit is greater among small firms, and that exporting firms and firms performing R&D activities enjoy better survival prospects. Görg and Strobl (2000) examine whether MNCs can impact positively on firm survival through technology spillover and negatively through crowding out effects. Applying the Cox proportional hazard model to data on Irish firms, they find that, after controlling for other firm and sector-specific effects, the presence of multinationals has a life enhancing effect on indigenous firms in high tech industries, suggesting the presence of technology spillovers. For the Indian pharmaceutical industry, a study of firm exit based on the Cox proportional hazard model has been undertaken by Chadha and Ying (2008). They have found that the survival of pharmaceutical firms in India has been adversely affected by Trade Related Aspects of Intellectual Property Rights (TRIPS) agreement after controlling for other firm characteristics such as size, experience, ownership, group membership and innovation. They also find that innovating firms have been able to survive the policy changes undertaken.

Turning now to the aspect of trade, Besedes and associates have undertaken several studies on export duration using the Cox proportional hazard model (see, for example, Besedes and Blyde 2010). Other studies that have used the Cox proportional hazard model in the context of trade include Bojnec and Ferto (2012), Rudi, Grant, and Peterson (2012) and Shao, Xu, and Qiu (2012). Chen (2012) has used the Cox proportional hazard model to examine the effect of innovation on duration of exports. Data on product level exports from more than 160 countries to the US market in the period of 1972–2006 have been considered for the analysis. The results indicate that innovation increases the duration of exports. It is also found that innovation shortens the export lag.

A paper by Cesaroni, Giarratana, and Martínez-Ros (2010) deserves a special mention because it deals with the entry of Spanish pharmaceutical firms into the US market (an issue similar to the one investigated in this paper). Data for the period of 1995–2004 have been used for the analysis and a hazard model has been estimated (a piece-wise exponential model specification has been applied, different from the Cox proportional hazard model). The results show that the technological capabilities of a firm (measured by the breadth and depth of the firm's patent base) and the cost structure of the firm explains its entry into the US market with a branded product.

3. Data, variables and preliminary analysis

3.1 *Data*

The basic data for the analysis have been taken from *Capitaline* (see www.capitaline.com). Data for the period of 1999–2000 to 2010–2011 are used for the analysis. In the *Capitaline* data-source, pharmaceutical companies have been divided into five groups: (1) Bulk drugs manufacturing domestic firms; (2) Bulk drugs and formulations manufacturing domestic firms – large; (3) Bulk drugs and formulations manufacturing domestic firms – medium and small; (4) Formulations manufacturing domestic firms and (5) Multinational firms. Data could be obtained for about 180–230 firms for different years in the period under study. This is an unbalanced panel and the firms included in the dataset vary from year to year. For about 30% of the firms, data are available for all 12 years. On the other hand, for another 30% of the firms, data are available for four years or less.

The information on the group to which each firm belongs has been used for constructing two dummy variables: one for the bulk drug manufacturers (i.e. group 1 above) and the other for multinational firms (group 5 above). As described later in the paper, these two groups differ from the other firms in terms of export intensity. The bulk drug manufacturers have relatively high export intensity while multinational firms have relatively low export intensity. It was important therefore to incorporate this aspect into the econometric analysis with the help of dummy variables.

3.2 *Variables*

From the *Capitaline* database, data on sales, production cost, exports, imports, R&D expenditure, invested capital, year of incorporation, foreign equity proportion, etc. for the pharmaceutical firms have been drawn (for the period 1999–2000 to 2010–2011). Using these data, the following variables have been constructed for the econometric analysis:

Export intensity: Ratio of exports to sales;

R&D intensity: Total expenditure on R&D as a ratio to sales;

Technology import intensity: Expenditure on royalty and technical fees paid in foreign exchange as a ratio to sales;

Age of machinery: A proxy formed by the ratio of cumulative depreciation to the gross value of fixed assets;

Bulk drug producer firm (dummy): dummy variable taking value one for firms engaged in the production of bulk drugs (not producing formulations) and zero otherwise; and

Multinational firm (dummy): dummy variable taking value one for multinational pharmaceutical firms and zero otherwise.

In addition to the variables listed above, the following variables have been constructed for the econometric analysis:

Foreign equity participation: The share of foreign equity out of the total equity of the firm forms this variable. There is difficulty in getting this information for each year under study. Thus, for each firm, the share of foreign equity has been computed for the latest year for which data are available, and then the ratio has been applied for all other years.

Post-1995 firm (dummy): This is a dummy variable which takes value one if the firm was incorporated 1995 or later. It takes value zero for firms that were incorporated before 1995. The firms which were set up after the new patent regime had been introduced may have a different orientation than those set up in the previous patent regime. The dummy variable is intended to incorporate this aspect into the analysis.

Technical efficiency: To estimate technical efficiency, a Cobb–Douglas stochastic frontier production function has been estimated. Since panel data are used for the estimation of production function, year dummies have been introduced in the estimation of the production function allowing the intercept to change over time (thereby capture, to the extent possible, technological change and other general inter-temporal changes). Sales deflated by the wholesale price index for drugs and medicine have been taken as the measure of output. Labour cost has been converted into a measure of labour input by dividing it by the wage rate. Emoluments per employee in the drugs and pharmaceuticals industry has been computed from data available in the *Annual Survey of Industries* (Central Statistical Office, Government of India), and this has been used to convert labour cost reported by firms into a measure of labour input. Expenditure incurred on power and fuel has been deflated by a price index of energy to obtain a measure of energy input. Wholesale price indices for coal, oil and electricity have been combined to form a price index of energy for the drugs and pharmaceuticals industry. The weights used are based on the relative magnitude of these inputs as given in the Input–Output table for 2003–2004 (published by the Central Statistical Office). In a similar manner, a price index for materials inputs for the pharmaceuticals industry has been formed. The reported cost of materials has been deflated by this price index to get a measure of materials input. Gross value of fixed assets deflated by the wholesale price index for machinery has been taken as the measure of capital input. When materials input was included in the estimated frontier production function, the estimates of technical efficiency showed very little variation across firms. Therefore, in the model finally applied, labour, capital and energy have been taken as three inputs, and real sales has been taken as a measure of output.

The estimate of frontier production function and the estimates of technical efficiency of firms obtained therefrom have some limitations. First, a blanket deflation procedure has been used for capital input which is inferior to the perpetual inventory method of constructing capital series. Second, the exclusion of materials input from the production function introduces a bias in the parameter estimate. But, it is hoped that the conclusions of the study do not get affected seriously by these inadequacies of technical efficiency estimates. Perhaps, even if more accurate estimates of technical efficiency were used, the results of the econometric analysis would not have been much different.

3.3 *Preliminary analysis*

Figure 1 shows the average export intensity of firms that ranked low in terms of R&D intensity, compared to the average export intensity of firms that ranked high in terms of R&D intensity. The

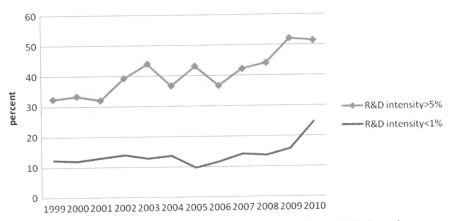

Figure 1.   Export intensity of pharmaceutical firms, classified according to R&D Intensity.
Source: Author's computation based on Capitaline database.

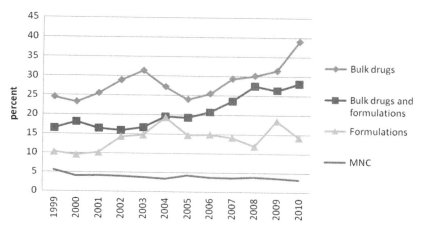

Figure 2. Export intensity of pharmaceutical firms, by type of firms.
Source: Author's computation based on Capitaline database.

former group includes firms in which R&D to sales ratio was less than 1%. The latter group includes firms in which the ratio in question was more than 5%. It is seen from the graph that the firms which have spent relatively more on R&D are also the ones which have directed a greater portion of the sales to export markets.

Figure 2 shows the average export intensity of firms, classified into four categories: (i) firms engaged in the production of bulk drugs, (ii) firms engaged in the production of bulk drugs and formulations, (iii) firms engaged in the production of formulations only and (iv) firms set up in India by MNCs. It is evident that the average export intensity is the highest for the first group and the lowest for the last group. Also, it is interesting to observe that the average export intensity of bulk drug manufacturers has increase over time, whereas that for MNCs had a slight fall.

Let us consider now the distribution of pharmaceutical firms according to the proportion of output they export. In 1999, about 10% of the pharmaceutical firms directed more than 50% of their sales to export markets. This proportion rose to about 20% of firms in 2010 (Figure 3). On the other hand, the proportion of firms that exported less than 1% of their output (including

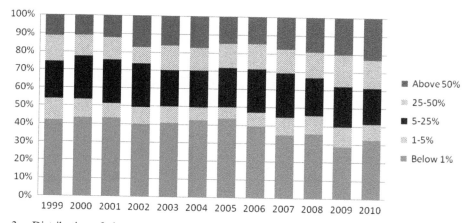

Figure 3. Distribution of pharmaceutical firms according to export intensity, 1999–2010.
Source: Author's computation based on Capitaline database.

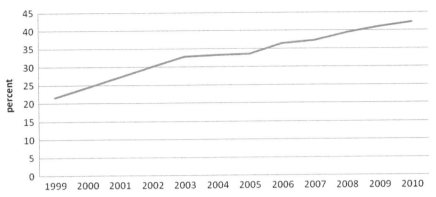

Figure 4. Export intensity, pharmaceutical firms (for which data are available all years).
Source: Author's computation based on Capitaline database.

those that do not export at all) has gone down between 1999 and 2010. The proportion was a little over 40% in 1999. It came down to a little over 30% in 2010.

Data on sales and exports obtained for the pharmaceutical firms reveal that export intensity increased from about 19% in 1999 to about 41% in 2010. Since the computed export intensity is affected by the entry and exit of firms, it is would be useful to examine the export intensity of firms for which data could be found for all 12 years under study. The export intensity computed for these firms is shown in Figure 4. The export intensity of this group of firms increased from about 22% in 1999 to about 42% in 2010. Within this group, about 18% firms exported more than 50% of their output in 1999. This proportion rose to 26% of firms in 2010.

4. Results of econometric analysis

The results of the regression analysis (Equations (2)–(4)) are presented in Table 1. As mentioned earlier, the data used for regression analysis relate to the period 1999–2000 to 2010–2011. Data for 319 firms are used. For only about 30% of the firms, data are available for the full period under study. This explains why the number of observations is 2273 when the number of firms considered is 319 and the period covered is 12 years.

It is seen from Table 1 that the interaction term between R&D and technical efficiency has a positive and statistically significant coefficient in all four regressions. This supports the hypothesis that R&D has a positive effect on export intensity and the effect goes up as the level of productivity of firm increases.[6]

Turning to other firm characteristics included in the model as explanatory variables, a significant positive effect of firm size on export intensity is indicated by the regression results. A significant positive effect is also found for foreign equity participation and technology import intensity. The age of machinery variable has a significant negative coefficient, which indicates that *ceteris paribus* a firm with relatively old plant and machinery would have lower export orientation. Such a relationship between export intensity and age of plant and machinery is expected. Interestingly, the results seem to suggest that a firm incorporated in the period since 1995 has lower export intensity than a firm incorporated earlier. To assess the robustness of this result, the cut-off date has been changed and the regressions re-estimated. When the cut-off is changed to 1997 or 2000, the coefficient remains negative but becomes statistically insignificant. Hence, not much importance should be given to the finding of a significant negative coefficient for this dummy variable. But, there is evidence to suggest that after controlling for other factors,

Table 1. Regression results, model explaining export intensity of pharmaceutical firms (No. of observations = 2273, No. of firms = 319, period 1999–2000 to 2010–2011).

Explanatory variable	OLS	Tobit	Tobit random effects (I)	Tobit random effects (II)
R&D intensity	−0.083 (−0.29)	0.333 (0.85)	−0.595 (−2.04)**	–
R&D intensity* technical efficiency	1.646 (3.40)***	1.258 (1.89)*	1.233 (2.53)**	0.329 (2.39)**
Technology import intensity	0.819 (2.22)**	1.065(2.24)**	0.916 (2.30)**	0.894 (2.29)**
Firm size	0.030 (10.39)***	0.066 (15.48)***	0.050 (13.09)***	0.050 (12.54)***
Incorporated in or after 1995 (dummy)	−0.063(−3.95)***	−0.128 (−5.58)***	–	–
Firm engaged in the production of bulk drugs (dummy)	0.090 (8.08)***	0.129 (8.50)***	–	–
Multinational firm (dummy)	−0.179(−7.74)***	−0.202 (−6.52)***	–	–
Age of machinery	−0.062(−2.00)**	−0.116 (−2.66)***	−0.177 (−3.33)***	−0.179 (−3.25)***
Foreign equity proportion	0.300 (5.21)***	0.211 (2.76)***	–	–
Year effects	Yes	Yes	Yes	Yes
Firm effects	No	No	Yes	Yes
R^2	0.21			
Pseudo R^2		0.30		
LR (χ^2)		679.6 (df=20)		
Wald χ^2			296.5 (df=16)	360.3 (df=15)
Likelihood ratio test for random effects; testing for $\sigma_u = 0$. Chibar-squared (df=1); P-value in square parenthesis			2271.99 [Prob ≥ chibar-squared = 0.000]	2268.65 [Prob ≥ chibar-squared = 0.000]

Source: Author's computation based on Capitaline database.
Note: For the foreign equity proportion, data for the latest available year are used. This variable, therefore, does not vary over time. Accordingly, in the random-effects Tobit model, this variable gets dropped. The same applies to the dummy variables.
*Statistically significant at 10%.
**Statistically significant at 5%.
***Statistically significant at 1%.

the firms which were set up after the introduction of the new patent regime were not more export oriented than those set up earlier, during 1970–1994.

The dummy variable for bulk drugs manufacturers has a significant positive coefficient while the dummy variable for multinational firms has a significant negative coefficient. This is consistent with the pattern observed in Figure 2. The results suggest that while multinational pharmaceutical firms operating in India are not inclined to exporting their products from India, the domestic firms with foreign equity participation are more export oriented than the domestic firm not having foreign equity participation.

For the estimates of the random-effects Tobit model, a test for random effects has been done. This is shown in the bottom row of Table 1. The null hypothesis is that σ_i is zero for all i. In other words, there is no firm-specific effect. This hypothesis is strongly rejected by the test. The implication is that there are firm effects and these need to be taken into account in the estimated model. Hence, the Tobit random-effects model is to be preferred.

Table 2. Estimated year effects, random effects Tobit model.

Year	Estimated coefficient of the dummy variable	t-Ratio
2000–2001	−0.002	−0.12
2001–2002	0.006	0.36
2002–2003	0.039	2.29**
2003–2004	0.047	2.71***
2004–2005	0.047	2.64***
2005–2006	0.026	1.44
2006–2007	0.022	1.20
2007–2008	0.023	1.22
2008–2009	0.034	1.76*
2009–2010	0.035	1.76*
2010–2011	0.041	2.01**
Test: $\delta_t = 0$; i.e. coefficients of all year dummies is zero. χ^2 (df = 11); P-value in square parenthesis	Chi-squared = 20.94 [Prob > Chi-squared = 0.034]	

Source: Author's computation based on Capitaline database.
Note: Coefficients of year dummies are shown in the table for the estimated Tobit random effect model (II) presented in the last column of Table 1.
*Statistically significant at 10%.
**Statistically significant 5%.
***Statistically significant 1%.

In the regression results presented in Table 1, the coefficients of the year dummies have been suppressed. These coefficients for Tobit random-effects model (II) are presented in Table 2. The year 1999–2000 is the base. Hence, the coefficients for other years, 2000–2001 to 2010–2011 are shown in the table. The estimated coefficients indicate that the year effects caused exports to go up between 1999–2000 and 2004–2005, following which there was a dip, and then there was an increase again. The null hypothesis that all coefficients of year dummies are zero is rejected by a test of this hypothesis which is shown in the bottom row of Table 2. At the same time, it should be noted that the size of the coefficients for 2009–2010 and 2010–2011 is small in relation to the increase that has taken place in the export intensity of pharmaceutical firms, by about 20 percentage points between 1999–2000 and 2010–2011. It seems therefore that year effects explain only small part of the increase in export intensity in Indian pharmaceutical firms that has taken place between 1999–2000 and 2010–2011.

4.1 Explaining entry into export market

The results of the Cox proportional hazard model are presented in Table 3. The results are by and large similar to those in Table 1. The results suggest that the probability of entering export market goes up with firm size.[7] The probability of entering export market is relatively higher for bulk drug producers and relatively lower for multinational firms as compared to other categories of pharmaceutical firms. These findings are in agreement with the results reported in Table 1. For technology import intensity and foreign equity participation, no significant effect is found in the Cox proportional hazard model. This is at variance with the results reported in Table 1. This might mean that technology imports and foreign equity participation do not have a strong impact on the firms' decision to enter the export market, but once a firm has entered the export market, these factors significantly influence the level of export intensity the firm is likely to reach.

From the results of the Cox proportional hazard model obtained, it appears that a higher level of R&D intensity tends to raise the probability of entering the export market. The interaction term

Table 3. Estimates of the Cox proportional hazard model, Indian pharmaceutical firms.

Explanatory variable	Model-1		Model-2		Model-3	
	Hazard ratio	z-Value	Hazard ratio	z-Value	Hazard ratio	z-Value
R&D intensity	31.586*	1.64			4.188***	3.22
R&D intensity * technical efficiency	0.034	−0.98	8.248***	2.73		
Technology import intensity	0.326	−0.18	0.280	−0.20	0.021	−0.64
Firm size	1.195***	8.76	1.187***	8.67	1.204***	10.03
Incorporated in or after 1995 (dummy)	0.709***	−3.03	0.700***	−3.14	0.729***	−2.91
Firm engaged in the production of bulk drugs (dummy)	1.203***	2.81	1.202***	2.80	1.216***	3.04
Multinational firm (dummy)	0.715**	−2.44	0.725**	−2.34	0.635***	−3.53
Age of machinery	0.647**	−2.12	0.632**	−2.24	1.036	1.01
Foreign equity proportion	0.997	−0.85	0.997	−0.86	0.998	−0.73
LR (χ^2)	157.2 (df = 9)		155.0 (df = 8)		169.9 (df = 8)	

Source: Author's computation based on Capitaline database.
*Statistically significant at 10%.
**Statistically significant at 5%.
***Statistically significant at 1%.

between R&D intensity and technical efficiency is also found to a have significant positive effect on the probability of entering export market. This is consistent with the regression results reported in Table 1, and lends support to the hypothesis that R&D efforts enhance export competitiveness, and the effect is greater for the firms that are closer to the technology frontier.

5. Conclusion

The export intensity of Indian pharmaceutical firms has increased substantially in the period after 1995 when the new, more restrictive patent regime was introduced in India. The hike in export intensity has been accompanied by an increase in R&D intensity of Indian pharmaceutical firms. The results of the analysis presented in the paper provide support to the hypothesis that increased R&D efforts of pharmaceutical firms was one of the important factors responsible for the observed increase in export intensity.

A second hypothesis put to econometric test is that the impact of R&D on exports depends on the level of productivity already reached by the firm. To put it differently, if a firm is close to the technology frontier, its R&D efforts will have a greater impact on its export competitiveness in comparison with a firm which is much below the technology frontier as reflected in its low level of productivity or technical efficiency. The econometric results presented in the paper provide support to this hypothesis.

The results of econometric analysis indicate a positive effect of firm size on the decision to export as well as the level of export intensity. Also, it appears from the econometric results that bulk drug manufacturers are more export oriented than firms engaged in manufacturing of formulations or both bulk drugs and formulations.

Acknowledgments

Comments and suggestions received from an anonymous reviewer are gratefully acknowledged.

Notes

1. There has been a good deal of research on the developments in the Indian pharmaceuticals industry in the period since 1995, dealing particularly with the response of the industry to the challenges of the new patent regime and the question of access to medicine (see Grace 2004; FICCI 2005; Dhar and Gopakumar 2006; Greene 2007; Jha 2007; Sampath 2008; Kiran and Mishra 2009; Goldar and Gupta 2010; Gopakumar 2010).
2. The reference here, as also later in the paper, is to the corporate sector firms. The corporate sector firms dominate in the total value of production of the pharmaceuticals industry.
3. Chaudhuri (2012) has studied the behaviour of multinational pharmaceutical firms in India in the post-TRIPS regime. He concludes that the days of product monopolies and high prices are back in India. The multinational firms have started marketing their new patented drugs at exorbitant prices particularly for life threatening diseases such as cancer. It may be pointed out in this context that Goldar and Gupta (2010, 111) have studied the prices of some patented drugs in recent years and have come to the conclusion that the foreign companies have not been able to (or are not willing to) price their patented drugs in India at the level of the reference price in other major markets.
4. Sampath (2008) observes that R&D investments in India's pharmaceuticals sector can broadly be split up into generics-related R&D and proprietary R&D for drug discovery research. The generics R&D is geared towards creating drug master files that are required to get approval in the US market for the sale of active pharmaceutical ingredients and to submit Abbreviated New Drug Applications that are a prerequisite to receive market approval for generic drugs. Such approvals are needed also for other regulated markets. Some of the companies that have been leading in terms of approvals received by Indian firms include Dr Reddy's Laboratories, Cipla Ltd, Max laboratories Ltd, Aurobindo Pharma Ltd and Ranbaxy Laboratories Ltd (Dhar and Gopakumar 2006).
5. Several studies have found evidence of self-selection of firms to export market based on their level of productivity. For Indian firms, such findings have been reported by Ranjan and Raychaudhuri (2011), Haidar (2012) and Thomas and Narayanan (2012), among others. Goldar and Kato (2009) have studied the export performance of Indian firms and have found empirical evidence that indicates that productivity of firms determines how import competition will impact the export intensity of firms. They conclude that while increased import competition is expected to raise the export intensity of high productivity firms, it may not have an effect or may have an adverse effect on the export intensity of low productivity firms.
6. In one of the regression equations estimated (Tobit random effects (I)), the coefficient of R&D intensity is negative and statistically significant. This, however, should not be treated as a sign of a negative marginal effect of R&D on export intensity because there is an interaction term involving R&D and technical efficiency, and the coefficient of the interaction term is positive and relatively bigger in numerical magnitude than the coefficient of R&D intensity. For the sample, the mean technical efficiency is about 0.64. Thus, at the sample mean, the marginal effect of R&D on export intensity is positive.
7. The estimated hazard ratio of this variable is more than one and the difference from one is statistically significant. It may, therefore, be inferred that as the size for a firm increases, it is more likely to turn into an exporting firm.

References

Aggarwal, Aradhna. 2004. "Pharmaceutical Industry." In *International Competitiveness & Knowledge-Based Industries*, edited by N. Kumar and K. J. Joseph, 143–184. New Delhi: Oxford University Press.

Bernard, A. B., J. Eaton, J. B. Jensen, and S. Kortum. 2003. "Plants and Productivity in International Trade." *American Economic Review* 93 (4): 1268–1290.

Besedes, Tibor, and Juan Blyde. 2010. "What Drives Export Survival? An Analysis of Export Duration in Latin America." Accessed May 30, 2013. http://siteresources.worldbank.org/INTRANETTRADE/Resources/Internal-Training/287823-1256848879189/Besedes_Mar16_2010.pdf

Bojnec, Stefan, and Imre Ferto. 2012. "Does EU Enlargement Increase Agro-Food Export Duration? *World Economy* 35 (5): 609–631.

Brenton, Paul, Christian Saborowski, and Erik von Uexkull. 2009. "What Explains the Low Survival Rate of Developing Country Export Flows?" World Bank Policy Research Working Paper No. 4951, World Bank, Washington, DC.

Bruno, Giuseppe. 2004. "Limited Dependent Panel Data Models: A Comparative Analysis of Classical and Bayesian Inference among Econometric Packages." Society for Computational Economics, Computing in Economics and Finance, No. 41. Accessed May 28, 2013. http://editorialexpress.com/cgi-bin/conference/download.cgi?db_name=SCE2004&paper_id=41

Cesaroni, Fabrizio, Marco S. Giarratana, and Ester Martínez-Ros. 2010. "US Market Entry by Spanish Pharmaceutical Firms." Working Paper No. 10-11, Business Economic Series 03, Departamento de Economía de la Empresa, Universidad Carlos III de Madrid, Madrid.

Chadha, Alka. 2009. "Product Cycles, Innovation, and Exports: A Study of Indian Pharmaceuticals." *World Development* 37 (9): 1478–1483.

Chadha, Alka, and Zhiliang Ying. 2008. "TRIPs, Innovation and Survival of Indian Pharmaceutical Firms." Paper presented at the 6th Annual International Industrial Organization Conference, Arlington, VA, May 16–18, 2008. Accessed May 30, 2013. https://editorialexpress.com/cgi-bin/conference/download.cgi?db_name=IIOC2008&paper_id=229

Chaudhuri, Sudip. 2005. *The WTO and India's Pharmaceutical Industry: Patent Protection, TRIPS and Developing Countries*. New Delhi: Oxford University Press.

Chaudhuri, Sudip. 2012. "Multinationals and Monopolies." *Economic and Political Weekly* 47 (12) March 24.

Chen, Wei-Chih. 2012. "Innovation and Duration of Export." *Economics Letters* 115 (2): 305–308.

Dhar, B., and K. M. Gopakumar. 2006. "Post 2005-TRIPS Scenario in Patent Protection in the Pharmaceutical Sector: The Case of the Generic pharmaceutical industry in India." Report, Geneva: UNCTAD, IDRC and ICTSD, November.

Esteve-Perez, Silviano, Amparo Sanchis Llopis, and Juan Alberto Sanchis Llopis. 2004. "The Determinants of Survival of Spanish Manufacturing Firms." *Review of Industrial Organization* 25 (3): 251–273.

FICCI. 2005. "Competitiveness of the Indian Pharmaceutical Industry in the New Product Patent Regime." (Report Submitted to the National Manufacturing Competitiveness Council). New Delhi: Federation of Indian Chamber of Commerce and Industry.

Goldar, Bishwanath, and Indrani Gupta. 2010. "Effects of New Patents Regime on Consumers and Producers of Drugs/Medicines in India." Revised Report Submitted to the UNCTAD. Accessed March 1, 2013. http://wtocentre.iift.ac.in/UNCTAD/09.pdf

Goldar, Bishwanath, and Atsushi Kato. 2009. "Export Intensity of Indian Industrial Firms in the Post-Reform Period." In *Indian Industrial Development and Globalisation: Essays in Honour of Professor S.K. Goyal*, edited by S. R. Hashim, K. S. Chalapati Rao, K. V. K. Ranganathan and M. R. Murty, 471–498. New Delhi: Academic Foundation.

Gopakumar, K. M. 2010. "Product Patents and Access to Medicines in India: A Critical Review of the implementation of TRIPS Patent Regime." *The Law and Development Review* 3 (2): Article 11.

Görg, Holger, and Eric Strobl. 2000. "Multinational Companies, Technology Spillovers and Firm Survival: Evidence from Irish Manufacturing." Research Paper 2000/12, Centre for Research on Globalisation and Labour Markets, School of Economics, University of Nottingham.

Grace, Cheri. 2004. *The Effect of Changing Intellectual Property on Pharmaceutical Industry Prospects in India and China: Considerations for Access to Medicines*. London: DFID Health Systems Resource Centre.

Greenaway, David, and Richard Kneller. 2007. "Firm Heterogeneity, Exporting and Foreign Direct Investment." *Economic Journal* 117 (517): F134–F161.

Greene, W. 2007. "The Emergence of India's Pharmaceutical Industry and Implications for the US Generic Drug Market." Office of the Economics Working Paper, No. 2007-05-A, U.S. International Trade Commission, Washington, DC.

Greene, William H. 2000. *Econometric Analysis*. 4th ed. (Indian Reprint, 2002). Delhi: Pearson Education (Singapore) Pte. Ltd., Indian Branch.

Gullstrand, Joakim, and Maria Persson. 2012. "How to Combine High Sunk Costs of Exporting and Low Export Survival?" Working Paper No. 2012/32, Department of Economics, Lund University. Accessed May 31, 2013. http://www.nek.lu.se/publications/workpap/papers/WP12_32.pdf

Haidar, Jamal Ibrahim. 2012. "Trade and Productivity: Self-Selection or Learning-by-Exporting in India." *Economic Modelling* 29 (5): 1766–1773.

Hess, Wolfgang, and Maria Persson. 2011. "Exploring the Duration of EU Imports." *Review of World Economics (Weltwirtschaftliches Archiv)* 147 (4): 665–692.

Hess, Wolfgang, and Maria Persson. 2012. "The Duration of Trade Revisited." *Empirical Economics* 43 (3): 1083–1107.

Holden, Darryl. 2011. "Testing for Heteroskedasticity in the Tobit and Probit models." *Journal of Applied Statistics* 38 (4): 735–744.

Jha, Ravinder. 2007. "Indian Pharmaceutical Industry: Growth, Innovation and Prices." PhD diss., Jawaharlal Nehru University, New Delhi.

Kiran, Ravi, and Sunita Mishra. 2009. "Changing Pragmatics of the Indian Pharmaceutical Industry in the Pre and Post TRIPS Period." *International Journal of Business and Management* 4 (9): 206–220.

Melitz, M. J. 2003. "The Impact of Trade on Intra-industry Reallocations and Aggregate Industry Productivity." *Econometrica* 71 (6): 1695–1725.

Melitz, M. J., and G. I. P. Ottaviano. 2008. "Market Size, Trade and Productivity." *Review of Economic Studies* 75 (1): 295–316.

Ranjan, Priya, and Jibonayan Raychaudhuri. 2011. "Self-Selection vs Learning: Evidence from Indian Exporting Firms." *Indian Growth and Development Review* 4 (1): 22–37.

Rudi, Jeta, Jason Grant, and Everett B. Peterson. 2012. "Survival of the Fittest: Explaining Export Duration and Export Failure in the U.S. Fresh Fruit and Vegetable Market." Paper presented at the Agricultural & Applied Economics Association's 2012 AAEA Annual Meeting, Seattle, Washington, August 12–14, 2012. Accessed May 30, 2013. http://ageconsearch.umn.edu/bitstream/124706/2/Rudi%2c%20Grant%2c%20Peterson%2c%20AAEA2012.pdf

Sampath, Padmashree Gehl. 2008. "India's Pharmaceutical Sector in 2008: Emerging Strategies and Global and Local Implications for Access to Medicines." A study commissioned by Department for International Development, UK.

Shao, Jun, Kangning Xu, and Bin Qiu. 2012. "Analysis of Chinese Manufacturing Export Duration." *China & World Economy* 20 (4): 56–73.

Thomas, Ronny, and K. Narayanan. 2012. "Productivity, Heterogeneity and Firm Level Exports: Case of Indian Manufacturing Industry." The 11th annual GEP Postgraduate Conference 2012, Leverhulme Centre for Research on Globalisation and Economic Policy (GEP), University of Nottingham.

Wooldridge, Jeffrey M. 2002. *Econometric Analysis of Cross Section and Panel Data*. Cambridge MA: MIT Press.

Appendix 1. Econometric issues

A.1 *Tobit model estimation*

The Tobit model for cross-section data may be specified as follows:

$$y_i^* = \beta' x_i + \varepsilon_i, \quad i = 1, 2, \dots N, \tag{A1}$$

$$\varepsilon_i \sim \text{NID}(0, \sigma^2),$$

$$y_i = y_i^* \quad \text{if} \quad y_i^* > 0 \quad \text{and} \quad y_i = 0 \quad \text{if} \quad y_{it}^* \leq 0.$$

In the model above, y^* is a latent variable (unobserved), while y is observed. The set of explanatory variables is denoted by x, and the corresponding parameters by β. The subscript i is for individuals. There are N observations. The error term is denoted by ε_i. The estimation of the parameters of the Tobit model is done by the maximum likelihood method. The likelihood function has two parts: a linear part and a Probit part. The likelihood function may be written as

$$L = \prod_{y_i=0} \left[1 - \Phi\left(\frac{\beta' x_i}{\sigma} \right) \right] \prod_{y_i>0} \left[\frac{1}{\sigma} \phi\left(\frac{y_i - \beta' x_i}{\sigma} \right) \right], \tag{A2}$$

where $\phi(.)$ is the standard normal density function and $\Phi(.)$ is the standard normal distribution function. The standard methods of maximization of log-likelihood yield the estimates of parameters, β vector and σ. The estimates of parameters have desirable properties.

The log-likelihood function for the random-effects Tobit model is, however, a complex expression. Consider the following model which is applicable to panel data:

$$y_{it}^* = \beta' x_{it} + u_i + \varepsilon_{it} \quad i = 1, 2, \dots, N, \quad t = 1, 2, \dots, T_i, \tag{A3}$$

$$u_i \sim \text{NID}(0, \sigma_u^2) \quad \text{and} \quad \varepsilon_{it} \sim \text{NID}(0, \sigma_\varepsilon^2),$$

$$y_{it}^* = y_{it} \quad \text{if} \quad y_{it}^* > 0 \quad \text{and} \quad y_{it}^* = 0 \quad \text{if} \quad y_{it}^* \leq 0.$$

The subscripts i and t are for individuals and time, respectively. The model allows for unbalance panel. The term u_i represents unobserved individual effects and measures heterogeneity among individuals.

For T_i observations for individual i, the likelihood contribution is given by the following expression (Bruno 2004):

$$L_i = \int_{-\infty}^{\infty} \left\{ \prod_{t=1}^{t=T_i} \left[\frac{1}{\sigma_\varepsilon} \phi\left(\frac{y_{it} - \beta' x_{it} - u_i}{\sigma_\varepsilon} \right) \right]^{d_{it}} \left[\Phi\left(\frac{-\beta' x_{it} - u_i}{\sigma_\varepsilon} \right) \right]^{(1-d_{it})} \right\} f(u_i, \sigma_i) du_i. \qquad (A4)$$

In the above equation, $d_{it} = 1$ for uncensored observation, and $d_{it} = 0$ for censored observation. $\phi(.)$ is the standard normal density function and $\Phi(.)$ is the standard normal distribution function. $f(u_i, \sigma_i)$ is normal density with mean u_i and standard deviation σ_i.

The likelihood function for the whole sample is the product of the contribution L_i over N individuals. Thus, the log-likelihood is obtained as

$$\ln L = \sum_{i=1}^{N} \ln(L_i). \qquad (A5)$$

The log-likelihood function in the above equation does not collapse to a sum as it would in the case of a time-series or a cross-section Tobit model.

In this study, STATA 8.0 has been used for estimating the random-effects Tobit model. This involves the following assumptions (Bruno 2004): (a) the idiosyncratic error ε_{it} is serially uncorrelated, (b) the individual effects u_i are uncorrelated across individuals and (c) $u_i|x_i \sim \text{NID}(0, \sigma_u^2)$. For estimating the random-effects model, STATA takes advantage of the Gauss–Hermite quadrature for the likelihood computation.

A.2 Heteroskedasticity in the Tobit model

In the presence of data censoring, the OLS estimator of linear models is biased and inconsistent. The application of the Tobit model yields consistent estimators in the presence of data censoring if the errors are normally distributed and are homoskedastic. However, if there is heteroskedasticity, the Tobit estimator is not consistent. This is regarded as a serious limitation of the Tobit model. Certain alternate modelling approaches have been suggested to get around the problem of heteroskedasticity in the Tobit model. These include Powell's censored least absolute deviation and symmetrically censored least squares.

Wooldridge (2002) has suggested a test of heteroskadasticity for the Tobit model based on an approach in which the standard Tobit model is nested in a more general alternative. Similarly, Greene (2000) has suggested a likelihood ratio test of a restricted model against one where the error distribution is allowed to vary across cases according to a specified relationship and a Lagrange Multiplier test. In a recent paper, Holden (2011) considers alternate tests for heteroskadasticity for a Tobit model and evaluates them by a Monte Carlo experiment.

STATA 8.0 which is the software used for the analysis presented in the paper does not contain a test for heteroskadasticity for the Tobit model. Nor does it provide heteroskadasticity corrected standard errors. The same applies to the random-effects Tobit model.

A.3 Estimation of the Cox proportional hazard model

The Cox proportional hazard model is a popular method of analysing the effect of covariates on the hazard rate. The hazard function is written as

$$h_i(t) = h_0(t) \cdot \exp(\beta' x_i). \qquad (A6)$$

In the above equation, x is the vector of covariates and β is the corresponding vectors of parameters. The subscript i is for individuals and t denotes time. The model is semi-parametric because the baseline hazard can take any form, while the covariates enter the model linearly. The estimation of parameters, β is done by the Cox's partial likelihood estimator. Suppose that the sample contains K distinct exit times, $T_1, T_2, ..., T_K$. For any point of time, T_i, the risk set R_i is all individuals whose exit time is at least T_i. In the simplest case in which exactly one individual exits at each distinct time and there are no censored observations, the partial log-likelihood is (Greene 2000)

$$\ln L = \sum_{i=1}^{K} \left[\beta' x_i - \sum_{j \in R_i} e^{\beta' x_j} \right]. \tag{A7}$$

Given the partial likelihood function, an estimate of the parameters may be obtained by maximization of partial log-likelihood.

The partial likelihood method of Cox described above is valid when survival time is a continuous variable and there are no ties (ties occur when two or more individuals exit at the same point of time). In empirical studies, these conditions are generally hard to meet. Since the individuals cannot be continuously monitored, ties in survival time are likely to arise. Consider the case in which two individuals exit at time T_i. The contribution to the log-likelihood is the sum of the terms for each of the individuals (Greene 2000). In such a situation, the approximations to log-likelihood suggested by Breslow or Efron may be used to get consistent and unbiased estimates.

While the use of the Cox proportional hazard model for analysing trade duration has been common, Hess and Persson (2012) point out several deficiencies of this approach. Some studies have used a discrete-time complementary log log (cloglog) model instead of the Cox proportional hazard model (for example, Brenton Saborowski, and von Uexkull 2009). But, according to Hess and Persson (2012), even this is not a good solution. They have recommended the use of discrete-time duration model such as logit and probit models with proper control for unobserved heterogeneity. In line with the advice of Hess and Persson, a random-effects logit model has been used by Gullstrand and Persson (2012). Similarly, Hess and Persson (2011) have used the discrete-time probit, logit and cloglog models in their study of duration of EU imports.

Mergers and acquisitions, technological efforts and exports: a study of pharmaceutical sector in India

Vidhisha Vyas, K. Narayanan and A. Ramanathan

Indian Institute of Technology Bombay, Mumbai, India

The paper attempts to examine the role of mergers and acquisitions (M&A) and technological efforts in determining the export competitiveness of firms belonging to the pharmaceutical sector in India. M&A provides synergistic gains to firms. New competitive advantages arise from the complementarities of merging and acquiring firms' specific intangible assets like production skills, brand names and better management capabilities. These gains could affect positively the export behaviour of domestic firms and increase their degree of internationalization. Technological efforts and other factors like firm size, age, multinational enterprise affiliation (MNEA) and capital intensity are also considered in the study. Two different econometric models, namely Tobit and Double Specification models are used for estimation and the results have been compared. The results of econometric exercise confirm that M&A, technological efforts, size and firm-specific characteristics are important in explaining export behaviour of firms.

1. Introduction

The relationship between technological efforts and international competitiveness is well documented in the literature in the context of both developed and developing economies. It is evident from the literature that trade theories explaining country-specific variables are insufficient to explain trade pattern and competitiveness. To fulfil this lacuna, firm- and market-specific characteristics have drawn the attention. A number of firm-specific characteristics have been identified in determining the trade and competitive behaviour of firms. These include firm size, age, choice of technology, imports, etc.

Many studies that have used export intensity as an indicator of international competitiveness explained the relationship between technological efforts and export behaviour (Posner 1961; Vernon 1966; Krugman 1979; Faberger 1988). Several studies have empirically validated that there exist a relationship between technological strategies and exports (Kumar and Siddharthan 1994; Wakelin 1998; Wignaraja 2002; Siddharthan and Nollen 2004; Bhat and Narayanan 2009). All these studies have by and large agreed that inter industry and inter firm variations could both be explained to a large extent by differences in technological strategies.

During the post-reform period, strategic decisions taken by firms influence their competitiveness. The global economic activities increasing foreign as well as domestic competition pushed firms to reconfigure their organizational structure and strengthen their core competencies (WIR

2000). Last two decades have experienced several waves of mergers and acquisitions (M&A) activity. In post-liberalization period, particularly in a country like India, the wave of industrial consolidation was unprecedented in terms of its size, sector involved, geographical coverage, etc. (Kumar 2000; Beena 2004; Pradhan 2007).

M&A helped firms to improve their position in domestic market and has given a fair chance to expand their business beyond the geographical boundaries. Firms acquire new competitive advantages by reaping synergistic gains like complementarity of firm-specific intangible assets such as production skills, marketing capabilities as well as enhanced and more efficient management capabilities. M&A also provide a firm with ample opportunities to capture new market gains overseas (Bertrand 2007).

These different motives assert that M&A could affect positively the export behaviour of the firms and their international presence could drive them towards being national champion. The possible impact of M&A on export competitiveness will determine whether policy-maker should or should not facilitate consolidation and the formation of national champions. It could be said that export enhancement should be the ultimate aim of national competitive policy (Geroski 2006; Bertrand 2007).

The pharmaceutical industry is chosen for the study as it is one of the oldest industries in India. Moreover, in Indian manufacturing industry, the maximum number of M&As have taken place in the pharmaceutical sector. The industry is classified as high-technology industry (OECD 2011) with the firms mainly producing generic drugs (branded and non-branded), intermediates and active pharmaceutical ingredients (APIs). Several technological activities are taking place in this industry. Therefore, this industry holds a strategic position in Indian manufacturing sector and expected to be technologically active.

The inward-oriented policy regime (1970–1991), abolition of product patents on food, chemicals and drugs in 1970 and permission for process patenting helped the development of a domestically competitive pharmaceutical industry in India. The imposition of price controls on certain formulations and bulk drugs discouraged the foreign participants, some of whom abandoned the Indian market. Forty years of protection has enabled this industry to grow significantly and to develop its research and manufacturing capabilities (Vyas, Narayanan, and Ramanthan 2012).

Deregulation and new product patent law of 2005 forced pharmaceutical firms to compete from within as well as from outside. Firms are adopting different corporate strategies like M&A and are taking huge efforts to acquire technological capabilities in order to remain competitive. Hence, there is a need to undertake a study investigating the relative importance of M&A and technological efforts in determining competitiveness of the firms in this leading industry in an emerging economy like India.

The remaining part of the paper is organized as follows. Section 2 provides theoretical background and the review of literature related to the study undertaken. Section 3 discusses the overview of M&A and exports in pharmaceutical industry in India. The Section 4 of the paper explains sample, variables and methodology used in the study. Section 5 provides the results and discussion on econometric analysis. The Section 6 presents the summary and conclusions.

2. Theoretical background and review of literature

2.1 *M&A and exports*

The present study attempts to investigate the impact of M&A on export behaviour of firms in Indian pharmaceutical industry. The linking of M&A and export is closely related to two main strands of the literature. A growing body of literature has analysed the determinants of international competitiveness, directly dealing with export intensity. In particular, numerous works have focused on the relationship between firm size and export intensity (Kumar and Siddharthan 1994; Wagner 2001; Bhat and Narayanan 2009). Recent studies emphasize the role of firm heterogeneity in understanding the export behaviour. In these lines, it could be said that experience and firms' home market performance are important for export activities. Firms even require some particular knowledge and skills to enter foreign market. Cost of exports could be lowered by advanced technological skills. Enhanced performance of firms in domestic market could transfer their local competitive advantages to foreign markets and boost exports (Bertrand 2007).

There is a parallel literature in industrial organization dealing with the incidence of M&A. Most of the studies examining the performance of merging and acquiring firms reached mixed conclusion. Theoretically, M&A allow firms to obtain three types of synergies, namely financial, operational and managerial synergies. Financial synergies are the one which lowers the cost of the capital for merged entities. They lower the systematic risk of a company's investment portfolio. M&A could lead to increase in the size of a firm giving it a better access to capital in comparison to smaller separate entities. Operational synergies develop by combining operation of two entities leading to economies of scale and scope. Economies of scale can be achieved by having a joint sales force or decrease in production cost or enable firm to offer unique products and services in the market by technology and knowledge transfers (Porter 1987). One more argument of M&A and export is market power consideration, which could encourage merging firms to increase their profits, by supplying less in the domestic market and exporting more.

Though M&A provides efficiency gains, the post integration organizational problem could thwart merging firms to reap the exact benefits. For example, firms could be plagued with longer delays with excessive cost of knowledge transfer and high rates of worker attrition. M&A can divert the manager's attention from vital activities like in-house R&D projects (Bertrand 2007). In the light of the above argument, it is difficult to state the clear effect of M&A.

A limited number of studies have explored the international dimension of M&A (Bertrand 2007; Mishra and Jaiswal 2012). Bertrand (2007) investigated the effect of domestic merger on export intensity in French manufacturing industry for the period 1992–1999. He concluded that export intensity of merging firms is not affected by domestic acquisitions. He also found that export intensity of buyer firms could improve but only in highly competitive industries. Mishra and Jaiswal (2012) using a panel of 33 Indian manufacturing industries for the period of 2000–2008 examined the impact M&A on export competitiveness of firms. Their findings suggest that industries with more M&A deals have greater penetration in international markets. The above literature specifies that there exists some relationship between M&A and export performance. As explained by national championship argument, there could be a positive relationship between export intensity and M&A (Bertrand 2007). Synergistic gains (in terms of cost) are usually specified by industrial organization literature and therefore, M&A could affect export behaviour of firms explained in a broadest sense.

2.2 *Technological efforts and export*

Departing away from the traditional Heckscher–Ohlin theory of trade with identical technologies among trading partners, Posner (1961) proposed technology gap theory. He asserted that countries with similar factor endowment can form differences in technical know-how as basis of trade. Extending this work, Vernon (1966) proposed product cycle theory and explained that countries can have comparative advantage in manufactured products by investing in new technologies and introducing new products to the market. Both these models predict that developed countries with high innovative capabilities would enjoy greater exports to developing countries. Nevertheless, with standardization of the products, the direction of the trade will reverse.

In case of developing countries, they were considered to be beneficiary of technology transfer from developed countries and the labour cost was basis of their comparative advantage. But this phenomenon was rejected on Japan's capabilities of inventing around a given technology, which tremendously boosted its competitiveness (Bhaduri and Ray 2004). Hence, technological capabilities acquired through various technological efforts turned out to be a major determinant of comparative advantage for developing countries (Siddharthan and Rajan 2002). Since technological capabilities are displayed majorly at the firm level, we tried to present a firm level model of export competitiveness in a high technology industry, namely pharmaceuticals. Indian pharmaceutical industry has acquired tremendous technological capabilities. The reverse engineering capabilities acquired by pharmaceutical firms has enabled the country to become self-reliant in health drugs as well as major exporter of generic drugs to overseas market of developed world (Bhaduri and Ray 2004).

The ways in which technological capabilities can be acquired by developing countries is through in-house R&D efforts, embodied and disembodied technology imports (DTIs), collaborations with foreign firms and very recently via M&A route. It is explained in the literature that development of technology is a cumulative endogenous process which is influenced by past innovative experience (Dosi 1988; Wakelin 1998). Developed countries firms' invest in R&D leading to new products and process development, which in turn boost export competitiveness of firms. But in the case of developing countries, this R&D is of rather adaptive in nature than innovative (Siddharthan and Nollen 2004).

The empirical evidences considering the effect of in-house R&D on exports is mixed. Few studies (Wakelin 1998; Basile 2001; Aggarwal 2002; Zhao and Zou 2002; Bhat and Narayanan 2009) found R&D to be positively and significantly impacting the export intensity. In the context of Indian pharmaceutical industry and electronics and electrical industry, Bhaduri and Ray (2004) found R&D to have a strong positive impact on exports. They asserted that large firms have huge R&D stock, it emerges as an important determinant of export performance.

Lall (2000) specified that developing countries like India gain competitive advantages in trade by importing technologies. Technologies can be imported either in embodied or disembodied form. Explicit or disembodied technologies are largely acquired by import of designs, drawings, blueprints and chemical formulas by paying royalty and technical fees. The empirical findings with regard to disembodied technology suggest mixed results again. Sterlacchini (1999) examined impact of innovation on export behaviour of non-R&D performing firms in Italian supplier dominated industries for the data of 1996. He found positive and significant impact of disembodied technology on exports. Siddharthan and Nollen (2004) examined the relation between MNE affiliation and exports for Indian information technology industry for the sample period 1994–1998, and found positive impact of disembodied technology on exports. However, for Indian chemical industry, Bhat and Narayanan (2009) and Kumar and Siddharthan (1994) do not find any statistically significant relationship between DTIs and exports performance.

Another way of acquiring foreign technology is through imports of capital goods and raw materials. The imported machines, new equipments and quality raw materials are considered to be embedded source of latest technology and modern designs. This help firms to improve their production process and produce quality products matching international standards. In the case of Italian manufacturing firms, Basile (2001) found that firms that achieved product and process innovation by importing new capital equipments have favourable impact on export performance. Sterlacchini (1999) on the similar lines studied the export behaviour of sub-sample of innovating firms in Italian manufacturing industry and found that expenditure in embodied technology exerts positive and significant impact on export intensity. Bhat and Narayanan (2009) examined the case of Indian chemical industry and found that capital goods imports are positively and significantly associated with export intensity. Siddharthan and Nollen (2004) found that embodied technology imports are one of the export determinants for domestic firms and unimportant for MNE affiliates. Aggarwal (2002) found positive relationship between imports of embodied technology and exports, for medium–high technology industries during the post-reforms era.

Import of raw material is another significant determinant of export behaviour for developing countries. Low tariff in post liberalization period facilitates import of raw materials which could make firms export competitive (Aggarwal 2002). Import of raw material from varied sources with different price and quality specifications can affect positively the exports to price competitive markets of developing countries and quality conscious markets of developed countries. Bhaduri and Ray (2004) confirmed that imports of raw material contribute positively and significantly to export intensity of pharmaceutical industry, but find no impact on electronics/electrical industry. Aggarwal (2002) also found positive and significant impact of imports of raw material in high technology industries as well as in medium–high and medium–low technology industries. Bhat and Narayanan (2009) concluded that import of raw material affect positively and significantly both decision to export as well as quantity of exports.

2.3 *Other firm-specific export determinants*

The following firm-specific determinants are considered as control variables in the present study.

2.3.1 *Firm size*

Size is one of the most commonly used variables in analysing export competitiveness. Size allows firms to achieve scale economies in production, marketing, R&D expenditure and reduce the international transaction cost. Large size firms with greater market power, better accessibility to resources and lower cost of financing the projects have advantage over smaller firms to exploit domestic as well as international markets.

Although empirical research reaches mixed conclusions, a positive relationship between firm size and exports is expected. Bonaccorsi (1992) reported mixed results in his review of research studies on size and exports relationship, but most studies emphasize on positive relationship between the two. Other international studies like Basile (2001) for Italian manufacturing industry, Zhao and Zou (2002) for Chinese manufacturing industry and Bertrand (2007) for French manufacturing industry found positive impact of size on export performance. In the case of Indian studies, Aggarwal (2002) for medium and low technology industries, Bhadauri and Ray (2004) for pharmaceuticals and electronics/electrical industries, Dholakia and Kapur (2004), Narayanan (2006) for automobile industry and Bhat and Narayanan (2009) for basic chemical industry obtained significant positive relationship between firm size and exports.

However, Athukorala, Jayasuriya, and Oczkowski (1995) for Sri Lankan manufacturing industry obtained the result showing positive impact of firm size on decision to export but no significant effect on propensity to export. Siddharthan and Nollen (2004) in a study of Indian IT industry have obtained different results. For the domestic firms, size turned out to be positively significant; while that for MNE affiliated firms, size is affecting negatively and licensee firms have no impact of size on their export performance.

2.3.2 *Firm age*

Another standard determinant considered for empirical studies on exports is age of the firm. Age specifies firms experience and also determines accumulated capabilities by firm over the period of time (Bhat and Narayanan 2009). Therefore, firm's age can positively affect export performance. But considering a developing country like India, younger firms have to compete with well established older firms for market share. In such a situation, they may prefer entering foreign market aggressively instead of competing in the domestic market. The empirical findings suggest mixed conclusion on relationship between age and export behaviour. Roberts and Tybout (1997) in the case of Colombian manufacturing industries and Majocchia, Bacchiocchib, and Mayrhoferc (2005) for Italian firms obtained a positive relationship between age and exports. Fryges (2006) for the studies of Germany and the UK, Bhaduri and Ray (2004) for Indian electronics/electrical industry and Bhat and Narayanan (2009) for Indian chemical industry observed that newer firms are more export intensive than their other counterparts.

2.3.3 *Advertising intensity*

Advertisement helps firm to create new market for their products as well as strengthen their position in existing markets. Firms create brand names by maintaining quality standards and enter foreign markets (Kumar and Siddharthan 1994). Kumar and Siddharthan (1994) and Willmore (1992) for Brazilian manufacturing firms found positive relationship between advertisement intensity and exports, but Bhat and Narayanan (2009) found that advertisement intensity affect negatively the export behaviour of firms in basic chemical industry.

2.3.4 *Capital intensity*

Role of factor intensity is also important in explaining export behaviour of firms. Capital intensity (CI) gives comparative advantage to firms by helping them to produce better quality and technologically superior products. But in country like India which is labour abundant firm might get competitive advantage in export market by adopting labour intensive technique of production. Bernard and Wagner (1996) for the German manufacturing industry, Athukorala, Jayasuriya, and Oczkowski (1995) for Sri Lankan manufacturing industry, Robert and Tybout (1997) for the case of Colombian manufacturing industry and Ozcelik and Taymaz (2004) in the case of Turkish manufacturing industry and Siddharthan and Nollen (2004) for Indian IT industry find CI to be positively impacting the export performance. On the other hand, Kumar and Sidharthan (1994) for six low and medium technology industries, Zhao and Zou (2002) for Chinese manufacturing industry and Bhat and Narayanan (2009) for Indian chemical industry obtained negative and significant relationship between CI and export behaviour.

2.3.5 *MNE affiliation*

Affiliation of firms to multinational enterprises gives them added advantage in export markets. MNE affiliated firms gain comparative advantage because of foreign parent's R&D capabilities, marketing and supplier network, financial resources and global brand names (Siddharthan and Nollen 2004). These characteristics allow MNE affiliated firms to exploit scale and scope economies and find new export markets. Siddharthan and Nollen (2004) found positive relationship between MNE affiliates and export intensity for Indian IT industry, on the contrary Bhat and Narayanan (2009) obtained significant negative impact of MNE affiliates on decision to export as well as on levels of exports for basic chemical industry in India.

2.3.6 *Leverage*

Availability of credit affects producers of different industries in different ways. Considering technological reasons, certain industries require more external funds for boosting exports. Credit affects both fixed and variable costs associated with exports (Manova 2008). Therefore, it could be argued that firm with higher leverage tend to export more, especially if they have borrowed from the market for the activities related to production and exports.

3. A brief overview of M&A and exports in Indian pharmaceutical industry

Liberalization facilitated Indian firms to market generics drugs to the USA and other Western European countries. Indian firms are aiming to move up the value chain by developing capabilities to produce super generics and branded generics. Indian companies have realized that to compete with the global pharmaceutical companies, even in the domestic market, they need new strategies and greater innovation. Identifying the growth of domestic and foreign demand, most Indian pharmaceutical companies aimed at expanding their manufacturing capacities mostly by means of M&A. Drive to get market access, new technologies, enhances the size and thereby attaining higher economies of scale could be considered as key motivations for M&A in pharmaceutical sector (Vyas, Narayanan, and Ramanthan 2012).

3.1   M&A in Indian pharmaceutical industry

In Indian pharmaceutical industry, 307 M&A deals have been undertaken in the given time period of 2000–2010. Out of the total deals, number of mergers is 89 (29%) and number of acquisitions is 218 (71%) (Figure 1). The deal value of total acquisitions for the period of 2000–2010 is Rs. 47,850.80 millions.[1]

In the pharmaceutical industry, out of the total acquisitions[2] concluded in the study period of 2000–2010, 54.58% (119 deals out of total acquisitions) are in the form of substantial acquisition of shares, while 16%t (35 deals) are in the form of minority acquisition of shares and 29.35% (64 deals) are in the form of acquisition of assets (Figure 2). Eighty per cent of M&A deals show horizontal consolidation. This explains that horizontal consolidation results in better synergistic gains in the pharmaceutical industry. Horizontal M&A allow firms to reap benefits of economics of scale, increased market share, reduced cost and lower competition (Basant 2000).

Economic reforms and deregulation of various government policies intensified the restructuring activities by undertaking different types of consolidation strategies. In the first half of 1990s, these activities are dominated by domestic M&A. But cross border transactions started becoming more prominent as there is an unprecedented rise in their numbers since mid-1990s, and it is still continuing (WIR 2010). In Indian pharmaceutical sector, 39% of the acquisitions are in the form

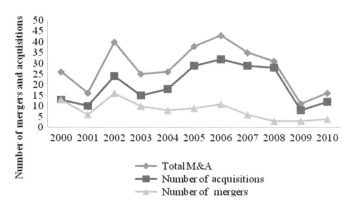

Figure 1.   M&A in Indian pharmaceutical industry 2000–2010.

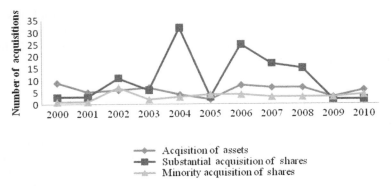

Figure 2.   Types of acquisitions in Indian pharmaceuticals industry 2000–2010.

of cross border deals and 61% are domestic deals. While in the case of mergers, all the deals are domestic in nature.

3.2   *Exports in Indian pharmaceutical industry*

Over 60% of India's bulk drug production is exported. The latest data specify that the amount of exports has increased to $5.1billion in 2010. Pharmaceutical industry contributes more than 2% in total exports for the entire study period of 2000–2010 (Figure 3). There are some fluctuations in initial year of study, but the share is continuously rising since 2006 and it is highest in the year 2009 (2.9%).

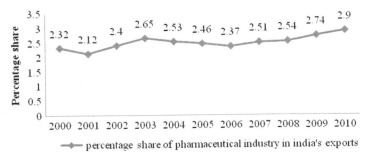

Figure 3.   Percentage share of pharmaceuticals industry in India's exports.

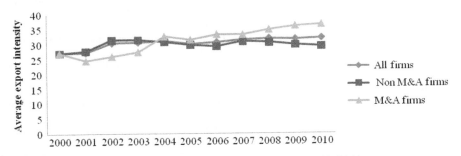

Figure 4.   Average export intensity of Indian pharmaceutical firms 2000–2010.

Figure 4 depicts that the average export intensity for the sample as a whole has been almost constant after 2005, but those of non-M&A firms is declining and that of M&A firms is increasing over the period of time. It is also interesting to observe that export intensity of M&A firms is nearly double to that of non-M&A firms in the year 2010.

4. Sample, variables and methodology

4.1 *Sample*

This section presents the data, description of variables and the methodology used in the analysis. The study uses panel data for the period from 2000 to 2010 for Indian pharmaceutical industry. The source of data for the firm characteristics is CMIE Prowess database version 4.0 accessed in the month of April 2012. The sample includes 161 firms, with a total of 1771 observations for 11 years. Table 1 presents the definition of variables and the method of constructing them.

4.2 *Methodology*

Export behaviour of a firm involves two decisions (Athukorala, Jayasuriya, and Oczkowski 1995; Wakelin 1998). The first decision is to choose to export or not. The second is to fix on what proportion of output to be exported. The data-set will include both exporting and non-exporting firms. The dependent variable, i.e. export intensity will frequently take a value of zero. For such a censored sample, OLS regression may not be the most suitable estimation procedure as coefficients will be biased towards censoring point (zero in present case).

A generally used approach to deal with the censored sample is Tobit model (Gujarati and Sangeetha 2007; Greene 2008). However, the Tobit model constraints the participation equation and the intensity equation to have similar set of explanatory variables and parameters. The Tobit

Table 1. Definitions of variables.

Sl. no.	Variable	Symbol	Definition used in the study
1.	Export intensity	EXPI	(FOB value of exports/net sales of the firm)*100
2.	R&D intensity	RDI	(Expenditure on R&D/net sales of the firm)*100
3.	Import of embodied technology (capital goods) intensity	ETI	(Expenditure on import of capital goods/net sales of the firm)*100
4.	Import of raw material	MRI	(Expenditure on import of raw material/net sales of the firm)*100
4.	Import of disembodied technology Intensity	DTI	(Lump sum, royalty, and technical fees payments in foreign currency/net sales of the firm)*100
5.	Age of the firm	AGE	Difference between the year in the study and the year of incorporation
6.	Firm size	Size	Natural log of the net sales
7.	Advertisement intensity	ADVT	(Expenditure on advertisements/net sales of the firm)*100
8.	Leverage	LEV	(Total borrowings of the firm/total assets of the firm)*100
9.	Capital intensity	CI	(Total assets/net sales)*100
11.	Dummy for merger and acquisition deals	DMA	Dummy = 1 for firms undertaking M&A activity, 0 otherwise
12.	Dummy for MNEA affiliation	DMNEA	Dummy = 1 for multinationals affiliated firms, 0 otherwise

Note: FOB, free on board.

model may be misspecified, in this case, leading to undesirable consequences for the estimates. This constraint can be relaxed by involving two separate equations. Cragg (1971) proposed a Double Specification model. The main feature of Double Specification model is that probability of exporting and quantity of exports are assumed to stem from two separate choices of firms and determinants of two decisions are allowed to behave differently. Therefore, the first part of Double Specification model using the whole set of data consider the probability to export. Probit model is appropriate for such kind of study. For the second part, only the subsets of sample selling abroad are considered. Hence, the truncated regression is an appropriate model where dependent variable is observed only if it is greater than zero.

Given the same set of variables affecting the probability of exporting and quantity to export, a likelihood ratio test (LR test)[3] (Greene 2008) can be used to test which of the two models is better. The present study compares the results on export performance of Indian pharmaceutical firms using Tobit model and Cragg's Double Specification model.

The Tobit model for export competitiveness can be specified as:

$$EXPI^* = \alpha_0 + \alpha_1\, AGE + \alpha_2\, SIZE + \alpha_3\, RDI + \alpha_4\, ETI + \alpha_5\, DTI + \alpha_6\, PROF + \alpha_7\, ADVI +$$
$$\alpha_8 LEV + \alpha_9\, CI + \alpha_{10}\, DMA + \alpha_{11} DMNEA + u_1. \tag{1}$$

$$EXPI = EXPI^* \text{ if } EXPI^* > 0$$
$$= 0 \text{ if } EXPI^* \le 0.$$

The Double Specification model nests the Tobit model as a special case.

The Probit model for probability of exporting can be expressed as follows:

$$DEXPI = \beta_0 + \beta_1\, AGE + \beta_2\, SIZE + \beta_3\, RDI + \beta_4\, ETI + \beta_5\, DTI + \beta_6\, PROF + \beta_7\, ADVI +$$
$$\beta_8\, LEV + \beta_9\, CI + \beta_{10} DMA + \beta_{11}\, DMNEA + u_2. \tag{2a}$$

$$DEXPI = 0 \text{ if firm does not export}$$
$$DEXPI = 1 \text{ if firm export.}$$

The second stage of Double Specification model, i.e. Truncation model can be specified as:

$$EXPI = \gamma_0 + \gamma_1\, AGE + \gamma_2\, SIZE + \gamma_3\, RDI + \gamma_4\, ETI + \gamma_5\, DTI + \gamma_6\, PROF + \gamma_7\, ADVI +$$
$$\gamma_8\, LEV + \gamma_9\, CI + \gamma_{10}\, DMA + \gamma_{11}\, DMNEA + u_3. \tag{2b}$$

Equation (2b) is estimated when $DEXPI = 1$.

4.3 *Empirical analysis*

4.3.1 *Descriptive statistics*

The differences in the mean of firm characteristics are highlighted for exporters and non-exporters in Table 2. Since the authors are expecting difference in the structure and behaviour of firms undertaking M&A and those not going for M&A, their means and standard deviations are highlighted separately in Table 3.

Table 2 highlights that mean export intensity of the sample is 21% but those of exporters are higher than that of full sample. The observations in the sample are fairly experienced with mean age of firms being 27 years. The mean intensity for technology variables is highest for raw material import intensity and lowest for disembodied technology intensity.

Table 2.   Descriptive statistics for full sample and exporting and non-exporting firms.

Variables	Full sample	Exporters	Non-exporters
EXPI	21.30 (25.55)	28.99 (25.81)	–
Age (in years)	26.67 (19.69)	28.36 (20.86)	21.97 (15.08)
Size (in Rs. millions)	519.04 (8.13)	1012.32 (5.98)	79.83 (5.41)
ADVI	1.078 (3.66)	1.11 (3.24)	0.986 (4.63)
RDI	1.831 (4.35)	2.26 (3.76)	0.635 (5.50)
MRI	9.77(13.56)	12.37 (14.31)	2.60 (7.50)
ETI	1.04 (4.79)	1.19 (4.99)	0.62 (4.17)
DTI	0.102 (0.57)	0.088 (0.397)	0.13 (0.88)
LEV	29.94 (34.34)	27.52 (22.30)	36.65 (54.86)
CI	230.49 (626.62)	152.89 (123.52)	445.31 (1173.30)
DMA	Number of observations that are performing M&A = 527 (30%)	Number of observations that are performing M&A = 476 (36.58%)	Number of observations that are performing M&A = 51 (11%)
DMNEA	Number of observations that have foreign affiliation = 165 (9.37%)	Number of observations that have foreign affiliation = 130 (10%)	Number of observations having foreign affiliation = 35 (7.44)
No. of observations	1771	1301	470

Note: Standard deviations are in parentheses.

Discussing the differences between exporters and non-exporters, we can observe that exporting firms are more experienced than non-exporting firms. The R&D intensity and advertisement intensity is higher for exporters. This shows that exporting firms invest more in advertisement to showcase their products in international markets. It is clear from Table 2 that exporters have higher raw material imports and higher embodied technology imports. The comparative higher R&D investment by exporters explains that in-house R&D facilitates faster the assimilation of technological imports.

Table 3.   Descriptive statistics for M&A and non-M&A performing firms.

Variables	M&A firms	Non-M&A firms
EXPI	29.90 (25.86)	17.65 (24.54)
AGE (in years)	33.37 (20.41)	23.82 (18.67)
SIZE (in Rs. millions)	7.98 (1.64)	5.52 (1.81)
ADVI	1.93 (4.57)	0.71 (3.13)
RDI	3.38 (4.50)	1.17 (4.11)
MRI	11.08 (11.83)	9.22 (14.20)
ETI	1.28 (2.51)	0.94 (5.48)
DTI	0.063 (0.22)	0.118 (0.66)
LEV	25.94 (20.19)	31.64 (38.69)
CI	231.12 (627.12)	230.23 (626.66)
DMNEA	Number of observations that have foreign affiliation = 99 (18.78%)	Number of observations having foreign affiliation = 58 (4.66%)
No. of observations	527	1244

Note: Standard deviations are in parentheses.

Table 3 clearly specifies that M&A firms are more export intensive than non-M&A performing firms. M&A undertaking firms are more experienced as well as larger in size. Such firms have higher advertisement and in-house R&D expenditure and they also tend to import more raw material and embodied technology. Also the percentage of firms having foreign affiliation is more in M&A group.

4.3.2 Correlation matrix

The correlation matrix in Table 4 reveals low levels of pair-wise correlation values among the variables. Technology variables have significant positive correlation with export intensity but of low order. Other firm characteristics like age, advertisement intensity and leverage and CI have statistical significant negative correlation coefficient with export intensity. However, it is generally found that cross-sectional studies suffer from the problem of heteroscedasticity (Gujarati and Sangeetha 2007). The Breusch–Pagan/Cook–Weisberg test reveals that the sample suffers from the problem of heteroscedasticity. Therefore, to get rid of this problem we have estimated the models using the robust[4] option available in the STATA 11 statistical package.

5. Econometric analysis, results and discussion

Table 5 presents the results for the two models discussed above. The LR test (Sterlacchini 1999; Greene 2008; Bhat and Narayanan 2009) conducted for the selection of the model suggests that, the Double Specification model (Probit + Truncation) is more appropriate than Tobit model for the present case. The results obtained for the truncated regression is akin to the estimates of random effect model. It is not possible to estimate fixed effect for truncated model in available software. Moreover, the objective of the paper is to distinguish between two groups of firms, M&A and non-M&A firms, and also to find the impact of cross-border M&A. To examine this one needs to classify the firms into groups rather than introducing firm heterogeneity. Therefore, random effect model of Tobit, Probit and Truncated regression is preferred for empirical analysis. The results also reinforce the idea that the effects of explanatory variable differ on the probability of exporting and on export intensity.

Table 5 also discusses the results of sub-sample of firms performing M&A and we found that for this sub-sample also Double Specification model is more appropriate in comparison to Tobit model. Therefore, the focus of the discussion would be on the results obtained using Double Specification model.

Table 4. Correlation matrix.

Variable	EXPI	AGE	SIZE	ADVI	RDI	MRI	ETI	DTI	LEV	CI
EXPI	1									
AGE	−0.07*	1								
SIZE	0.34*	0.29*	1							
ADVI	−0.13*	0.15*	0.08*	1						
RDI	0.24*	0.003	0.32*	−0.012	1					
MRI	0.45*	−0.02	0.32*	−0.06*	0.10*	1				
ETI	0.107*	−0.008	0.059*	−0.02	0.07*	0.004	1			
DTI	−0.02	0.009	−0.05*	−0.01	−0.01	−0.05*	−0.02	1		
LEV	0.005	−0.18*	−0.11*	−0.12*	−0.04	−0.02	−0.005	−0.02	1	
CI	−0.07*	0.04	−0.27*	0.06*	−0.0004	−0.10*	0.05*	−0.01	0.03	1

Note: Values with stars show significance level at 1% or more.

5.1 *Determinants of probability of exporting*

The results indicate that coefficient of M&A is positive and significant. Nevertheless, majority of M&A are in domestic market but M&A make firms outward looking for selling their products. The operational and financial synergies offered by the target reinforce firms' exporting capacity. Considering only the sub-sample of firms performing M&A, we have observed from the sample that all the firms going for cross border M&A are exporters[5] therefore, along with other factors cross-border M&A favours firm's decision to export.

Discussing the technological variables, results show that in-house R&D (RDI) favourably affects probability of exporting for full sample as well as for M&A firms though the results are insignificant in case of full sample. Import of raw material plays a positive and significant role in firms' probability of exporting for full sample as well as for M&A performing firms. Imports of embodied and disembodied technology have no effect on firms' probability of exporting in pharmaceutical industry.

As postulated and in line of findings of many other studies, size (SIZE) of the firm positively determines whether a firm will export or not. In pharmaceutical industry, production of generic drugs in bulk enables large firms to reap benefits of economies of scale. Firms that undertake large-scale production may find it necessary to expand to the overseas markets as production might be more than the domestic demand. Effect of size is insignificant in the case of M&A firms. Age specifies firms' experience and also determines accumulated capabilities by firm over the period of time. The coefficient of age (AGE) is positive but statistically significant only for merging and acquiring firms. It is evident from the results that older and more experienced firms, generally, possess higher probability of selling abroad. Our results differ with those of previous studies like Bhat and Narayanan (2009) and Fryges (2006), but matches with those of Roberts and Tybout (1997) and Majocchia, Bacchiocchib, and Mayrhoferc (2005).

MNE affiliation of firms (MNEA) is negatively impacting firms' probability of exporting for full sample as well as for M&A firms. Affiliated firms are in a better position to capture large shares in domestic markets itself, i.e. affiliation promotes firms to become inward looking. Also, MNEs may be entering India through the collaborative route to capture domestic market. These collaborations as a result may compel the domestic firms to increase domestic market share at the cost of exports. Advertisement intensity (ADVI) is having no impact on full sample, but for M&A firms advertisement investment helps firm to enter in overseas market as it help in creating brand value for the firm. Advertisement intensity is also a proxy for product differentiation and thus helps firms in showcasing their products internationally.

Leverage (LEV) deters firms to enter international market, but for M&A firms it plays a positive significant role in probability of exporting. Positive sign on leverage specifies that, in post M&A phase, firms might have better access to financial markets. M&A enables firms to reap benefits of scale and scope which can make them internationally competitive. Thus, they require funds in order to enter international markets. CI is negatively affecting firms' probability of exporting.

5.2 *Determinants of export intensity*

The results clearly indicate that M&A is contributing positively to improve the propensity to export. The coefficient of M&A is positive and statistically significant for the full sample. This result is similar to those of Mishra and Jaiswal (2012) who found in their study a positive impact of M&A on exports. Beena (2008) also found positive impact of M&A on export intensity in post-M&A period. Bertrand (2007) in his study of French manufacturing industry concluded no impact of domestic M&A on export intensity. In our sample of only M&A performing firms, the results indicate that cross border acquisitions boost exports significantly. Cross border M&A

Table 5. Panel data estimation of Tobit, Probit and Truncated models.

Variables	Full sample			Mergers and acquisitions		
	Models					
	Double Specification			Double Specification		
	Tobit (Robust)	Probit (Robust)	Truncated (Robust)	Tobit (Robust)	Probit (Robust)	Truncated (Robust)
Constant	-19.78^a (−6.26)	-1.78^a (−10.71)	-50.48^a (−4.61)	8.14 (1.26)	-1.45^a (−3.10)	25.70^b (2.42)
MA	6.90^a (4.27)	0.186^c (1.65)	15.11^a (3.59)	−	−	−
CBMA	−			5.14^b (2.17)	−	7.65^a (2.59)
MNEA	-17.80^a (−8.12)	-1.20^a (−7.62)	-28.90^a (−2.64)	-4.38^c (1.93)	-0.93^b (−2.27)	−6.71 (−1.38)
AGE	-0.122^a (−3.38)	0.0024 (1.10)	-0.28^b (−2.43)	−0.063 (−1.44)	0.038^a (3.70)	-0.172^b (−2.40)
SIZE	4.91^a (8.48)	0.40^a (12.23)	2.41^c (1.72)	0.420 (0.51)	0.061 (0.64)	−1.55 (−1.39)
ADVI	-0.60^a (−3.86)	0.012 (1.44)	-9.92^a (−5.76)	−0.241 (−1.63)	0.132^a (4.52)	-3.10^a (−4.19)
RDI	0.63^b (2.06)	0.008 (0.88)	2.47^a (6.93)	1.370^a (5.90)	0.337^b (2.07)	1.47^a (5.23)
MRI	0.80^a (13.49)	0.035^a (6.35)	1.32^a (12.38)	1.257^a (12.95)	0.080^a (2.60)	1.31^a (11.53)
ETI	0.48^b (2.39)	0.006 (0.82)	0.384^c (1.83)	0.922^a (3.07)	−0.015 (−0.60)	1.27^a (4.23)
DTI	1.52 (0.92)	0.007 (0.15)	9.32^a (2.96)	−3.90 (−1.22)	0.431 (0.96)	-31.72^c (−1.83)
LEV	−0.03 (−0.87)	-0.004^b (−2.20)	0.56 (0.52)	0.038 (0.76)	0.018^a (3.08)	−0.079 (−1.02)
CI	−0.002 (−1.63)	-0.0001^a (−2.71)	0.096^a (7.27)	-0.0059^b (−2.56)	-0.0009^a (−4.50)	0.013 (1.45)
No. of observations	1771	1771	1301	527	527	476
Log-LR	−6391.231	−670.327	−5483.390	−2095.223	−85.040	−1917.90
F-statistics/Wald χ^2	82.16^a	372.03^a	312.62^a	91.45^a	80.36^a	441.10^a

Note: Values in the parentheses are t-statistics for Tobit model and z-statistics for Probit and Truncated models.
[a]Significance level at 1%.
[b]Significance level at 5%.
[c]Significance level at 10%.

provide firms an opportunity to capture international markets by acquiring the target's tacit knowledge, brand names, access to better financial resources and managerial skills. Hence, the synergies offered by foreign targets boost exports of the firms.

Considering the impact of technological variables, in-house R&D effort (RDI), import of raw materials (MRI) and embodied technological imports (ETI) turn out more vital for the firms to enter the export market. It could be inferred that firms' rigorous in-house R&D along with import of latest technology can enable them to launch new and better products in the market. Indian pharmaceutical industry produces and exports majorly generic drugs and APIs. Production of these drugs largely depends on process development and reverse engineering which is supported by in-house R&D. For pharmaceutical industry, raw materials in the form of basic chemical are most important ingredient to produce API and generic drugs. At the same time, new ready to use plant and machinery can enable firms to produce improved quality of products. In post-liberalized era, pharmaceutical firms can import raw materials as well as capital goods from varied sources at different prices and of different qualities. Therefore, in-house R&D, import of raw materials and embodied technology boost pharmaceutical exports to quality seeking developed countries as well as to price sensitive markets of emerging economies (Bhaduri and Ray 2004).

However, DTI seem to affect positively and significantly the export intensity for the full sample only. It is negatively affecting the export intensity of M&A firms. It is expected that M&A firms acquiring abroad also acquire tacit knowledge as well as R&D and production capabilities of the target firms. Such firms by reaping the benefits of synergies can use the target location for exports. Thus, the results suggest that M&A firms do not require imports of disembodied technology to improve their export performance; rather it could be used to improve domestic sales. At the same time, since the full sample includes non-M&A performing firms, the import of disembodied technology assist them in the production of quality drugs using new and improved chemical compositions which take time to boost exports.

The age of the firm (AGE) appears to be an important factor in determining export intensity of pharmaceutical firms. The Double Specification model suggests that younger firms are more export intensive as compared to older firms. In liberalized regime, where full capacity production is now permitted, many established firms undertake high-scale production. This leads to excess supply in domestic market. Therefore, newer firms entering the industry with latest technology and better production skills find it easier to penetrate export market than to supply domestically (Bhat and Narayanan 2009). Another significant variable affecting export intensity is size (SIZE). For full sample, large size firm boosts exports because they can take advantage of economies of scale. But size turns out to be insignificant in affecting export behaviour of M&A undertaking firms.

Though advertisement and sales promotion is required for firms to showcase their products in international market, but for exporting firms in pharmaceutical industry, higher investment on advertisement (ADVI) do not lead to improved export performance. Indian pharmaceutical industry produce generic drugs and API in bulk, which are sold in international market by names of chemical composition, therefore, there is less scope of product differentiation. Hence, an aggressive advertisement strategy will only add to cost of production which will have a negative impact on exports. At the same time advertisement expenditure can create demand in the domestic market and therefore, in order to reduce export-related costs firm may choose to sell more in domestic market.

MNE affiliation (MNEA) turns out to be negatively impacting the export performance. Foreign firms collaborate with Indian firms keeping in view market seeking motive rather than efficiency seeking (Kumar 2000). Indian pharmaceutical firms have expertise in producing generic drugs via reverse engineering; therefore, it is possible that MNE enter Indian market with the motive of producing generic version of some branded drugs whose patents are soon to expire. This probably increases the dominance of affiliated firms in domestic market and may drive unaffiliated firms to seek new markets in foreign countries. Leverage (LEV) is having no impact on export behaviour of pharmaceutical firms, while CI is positively influencing export intensity of firms.

6. Summary and conclusions

This paper attempts to analyse the role of M&A and technological efforts in determining the interfirm differences in export intensity for a sample of firms drawn from the Pharmaceutical sector in

India. M&A appeared to affect significantly the export behaviour of pharmaceutical firms. Considering the full sample, it is evident that M&A influence positively the probability of exporting as well as the export intensity. Cross-border deals also drive firms to participate in export market and it does boost their export intensity. Therefore, we can suggest that M&A enhances pharmaceutical firms' efficiency and their export competitiveness in international market.

The results indicate that acquisition of technological capabilities either by in-house R&D or through imports of embodied or disembodied technology is an important determinant of firms' competitiveness in international market. In the pharmaceutical industry, acquisition of technological capabilities from abroad may not ensure better export performance unless it is acquired and assimilated efficiently (Bhaduri and Ray 2004). Here, sustained R&D is required for reverse engineering (for producing mainly generic drugs) to contend effectively in price competitive export market. Based on the source of procurement, import of embodied technology in the form of capital equipments and import of raw material help Indian pharmaceutical firms to take advantage of both price and quality competitiveness. In the case of disembodied technology, while it affects favourably the export performance of firms for the complete sample, it does not help boost exports of the sub-sample of M&A firms.

Apart from M&A and technological variables, we observed that firm size boosts export intensity. Another significant impact is that of age. There is clear evidence that younger firms are more successful in the export market. Since the domestic market is already being captured by more experienced firms, newer firms look forward towards foreign market to remain in the industry. In the case of M&A sample, however, firms' age has positive impact on probability of exporting. Advertisement intensity and MNE affiliation do not appear to help boost exports from this industry.

As a concluding remark it could be mentioned that in order to promote exports and to improve international competitiveness of domestic firms, competition policy (especially for M&A) could be formulated in such a way that it supports the argument of national champion. Another way of boosting exports is by subsidizing the technological efforts of firm in the emerging areas of industry. The government must provide incentive to those firms which are venturing into new product R&D, jointly with research institutions and other firms. Since, CI has negative impact on probability of exporting and has no impact on quantity of exports, efforts should be made to design policy which supports development of indigenous capital equipment and facilitate training and development of human resource. Similar studies should be conducted for other high technology intensive industries for better understanding the impact of M&A and technological efforts on export as well as for generalizing the results.

Acknowledgements

We gratefully acknowledge very useful comments and suggestions received from Prof. N.S. Siddharthan, two anonymous referees and participants of the seventh annual conference of the Knowledge Forum on the earlier draft of the paper. The errors that remain are our own.

Notes

1. Deal value is not reported for all acquisitions deals in CMIE Prowess database.
2. CMIE (Centre for Monitoring Indian Economy) segregates mergers and acquisitions data in the form of substantial acquisition of shares by acquirers (when 15% or more stake is purchased), minority acquisition of shares by acquirers (5% or more shares are purchased), acquisition of assets (acquire either a brand of the company or one of its plants or divisions or intangible assets) and merging with another companies.
3. Likelihood ratio test $\lambda = 2$(Ln Probit + LnTruncation − Ln Tobit), where Ln is the log-likelihood ratios. If λ is greater than the critical value of the chi-square distribution for the relevant degree of freedom, the

unrestricted model specification based on the combination of Probit and Truncated regressions is more suitable than the restricted Tobit model.
4. Robust term suggests heteroscedasticity corrected variance and standard errors.
5. Variable CBMA has not been used in Probit model of M&A sub-sample because all firms participating in cross-border M&A are present in export market.

References

Aggarwal, A. 2002. "Liberalisation, Multinational Enterprises and Export Performance: Evidence from Indian Manufacturing." *Journal of Development Studies* 38 (3): 119–137.

Athukorala, P., S. Jayasuriya, and E. Oczkowski. 1995. "Multinational Firms and Export Performance in Developing Countries: Some Analytical Issues and New Empirical Evidence." *Journal of Development Economics* 46 (1): 109–122.

Basant, R. 2000. "Corporate Response to Economic Reforms." *Economic and Political Weekly* 35 (10): 813–822.

Basile, R. 2001. "Export Behaviour of Italian Manufacturing Firms over the Nineties: The Role of Innovation." *Research Policy* 30 (8): 185–1201.

Beena, P. L. 2004. "Towards Understanding Merger-wave in Indian Corporate Sector: A Comparative Perspective." Working Paper No. 355, Center for Development Studies, Thiruvananthapuram, India.

Beena, P. L. 2008. "Trends and Perspectives on Corporate Mergers in Contemporary India." *Economic and Political Weekly* 43 (39): 48–56.

Bernard, A. B., and J. Wagner. 1996. "Exports and Success in German Manufacturing." Working Paper No. 96-10, MIT, Department of Economics.

Bertrand, O. 2007. "Domestic Acquisitions and Firm Level Export Intensity: Some Evidence on the National Champion Argument." CESifo Conference Paper, Munich.

Bhaduri, S., and A. S. Ray. 2004. "Exporting through Technological Capability: Econometric Evidence from India's Pharmaceutical and Electrical/Electronics Firms." *Oxford Development Studies* 32 (1): 87–100.

Bhat, S., and K Narayanan. 2009. "Technological Efforts, Firm Size and Exports in the Basic Chemical Industry in India." *Oxford Development Studies* 37 (2): 145–169.

Bonaccorsi, A. 1992. "On the Relationship between Firm Size and Export Intensity." *Journal of International Business Studies* 23 (4): 605–635.

"Centre for Monitoring Indian Economy (CMIE)." online Prowess 4.0 database accessed on April 2012.

Cragg, J. 1971. "Some Statistical Models for Limited Dependent Variables with Application to the Demand for Durable Goods." *Econometrica* 39 (5): 829–844.

Dholakia, R. H., and D. Kapur. 2004. "Determinants of Export Performance of Indian Firms – A Strategic Perspective." IIM A Working Papers, Indian Institute of Management, Ahemdabad.

Dosi, G. 1988. "Sources, Procedures and Microeconomic Effects of Innovation." *Journal of Economic Literature* 26 (3): 1120–1171.

Faberger, J. 1988. "International Competitiveness." *Economic Journal* 98 (391): 355–374.

Fryges, H. 2006. "Hidden Champions-How Young and Small Technology-oriented Firms can Attain High Export-sales Ratios." ZEW Discussion Papers 06–45, Germany.

Geroski, P. 2006. "Competition Policy and National Champions." In *Essays in Competition Policy*, edited by P. Geroski, 37–42. London: Competition Commission.

Greene, W. 2008. *Econometric Analysis*. Delhi: Pearson Education Asia.

Gujarati, D. N., and Sangeetha. 2007. *Basic Econometrics*. New Delhi: McGraw-Hill, Inc.

Krugman, P. 1979. "A Model of Innovation, Technology Transfer and the World Distribution of Income." *Journal of Political Economy* 87 (2): 253–266.

Kumar, N. 2000. "Mergers and Acquisitions by MNEs: Patterns and Implications." *Economic and Political Weekly* 35 (32): 2851–2858.

Kumar, N., and N. S. Siddharthan. 1994. "Technology, Firm Size and Export Behaviour in Developing Countries: The Case of Indian Enterprises." *The Journal of Development Studies* 31 (2): 289–309.

Lall, S. 2000. "The Technological Structure and Performance of Developing Country Manufactured Exports." *Oxford Development Studies* 28 (3): 337–367.

Majocchia, A., E. Bacchiocchib, and U. Mayrhoferc. 2005. "Firm Size, Business Experience and Export Intensity in SMEs: A Longitudinal Approach to Complex Relationships." *International Business Review* 14 (6): 719–738.

Manova, K. 2008. "Credit Constraints, Heterogenenous Firms, and International Trade." NBER Working Paper No. 14531, National Bureau of Economic Research, Cambridge, MA.

Mishra, P., and N. Jaiswal. 2012. "Mergers & Acquisitions and Export Competitiveness: Experience of Indian Manufacturing." *Journal of Competitiveness* 4 (1): 3–19.

Narayanan, K. 2006. "Technology Acquisition and PRIVATE Export Competitiveness: Evidence from Indian Automobile Industry." In *India: Industrialization in a Reforming Economy*, edited by S. D. Tendulkar, A. Mitra, K. Narayanan, and D. K. Das, 439–470. New Delhi: Academic Foundation.

OECD. 2011. ISIC Rev. 3" Technology Intensity Definition (OECD, online document). http://www.oecd.org/dataoecd/43/41/48350231.pdf

Ozcelik, E., and E. Taymaz. 2004. "Does Innovativeness Matter for International Competitiveness in Developing Countries? The Case of Turkish Manufacturing Industries." *Research Policy* 33 (3): 409–424.

Porter, M. E. 1987. "From Competitive Advantage to Corporate Strategy." *Harvard Business Review* 65 (3): 43–59.

Posner, M. V. 1961. "Technological Change and International Trade." *Oxford Economic Papers* 13 (3): 323–341.

Pradhan, J. P. 2007. "Trends and Patterns of Overseas Acquisitions by Indian Multinationals." Working Paper No. 10, ISID, New Delhi.

Roberts, M. J., and J. R. Tybout. 1997. "The Decision to Export in Colombia: An Empirical Model of Entry with Sunk Costs." *The American Economic Review* 87 (4): 545–564.

Siddharthan, N. S., and S. Nollen. 2004. "MNE Affiliation, Firm Size and Exports Revisited: A Study of Information Technology Firms in India." *The Journal of Development Studies* 40 (6): 146–168.

Siddharthan, N. S., and Y. S. Rajan. 2002. *Global Business, Technology and Knowledge Sharing: Lessons for Developing Country Enterprises*. Delhi: Macmillan.

Sterlacchini, A. 1999. "Do Innovative Activities Matter to Small Firms in Non-R&D-Intensive Industries? An Application to Export Performance." *Research Policy* 28 (8): 819–832.

Vernon, R. 1966. "International Investment and International Trade in the Product Life Cycle." *The Quarterly Journal of Economics* 80 (2): 190–207.

Vyas, V., K. Narayanan, and A. Ramanthan. 2012. "Determinants of Mergers and Acquisitions in Indian Pharmaceutical Industry." *Eurasian Journal of Business and Economics* 5 (9): 79–102.

Wagner, J. 2001. "A Note on the Firm Size: Export Relationship." *Small Business Economics* 17 (4): 229–237.

Wakelin, K. 1998. "Innovation and Export Behaviour at the Firm Level." *Research Policy* 26 (7): 829–841.

Wignaraja, G. 2002. "Firm Size, Technological Capabilities and Market-Oriented Policies in Mauritius." *Oxford Development Studies* 30 (1): 87–104.

Willmore, L. 1992. "Transnationals and Foreign Trade: Evidence from Brazil." *The Journal of Development Studies* 28 (2): 314–335.

WIR (World Investment Report). 2000. *Cross-border Mergers and Acquisitions and Development*. New York: UNCTAD.

WIR (World Investment Report). 2010. *Investing in A Low Carbon Economy*. New York: UNCTAD.

Zhao, H., and S. Zou. 2002. "The Impact of Industry Concentration and Firm Location on Export Propensity and Intensity: An Empirical Analysis of Chinese Manufacturing Firms." *Journal of International Marketing* 10 (1): 52–71.

Innovation and competitiveness among the firms in the Indian automobile cluster

Rahul Z. More and Karuna Jain

SJM School of Management, IIT Bombay, Mumbai, India

Automobile original equipment manufacturers are expanding their production bases to emerging economies to expand their market reach and leverage the existing capacity for auto-component manufacturing and provide opportunities for suppliers and subcontractors to build innovation capabilities leading to better performance. The innovation systems perspective and global value chain perspective contributes to develop important framework for evaluating innovation performance and maintain competitiveness of firms. These firms utilize external source of innovation and knowledge spillover externalities at cluster. This study explores firm's innovation capabilities and economic performance in the Indian automobile cluster. Empirical evidence shows that how firms can interact with Innovation Systems and Global Value Chains to build innovation capabilities (technological capability, manufacturing capability, organizational capability, strategic planning capability and marketing capability). The structured equation modeling has been performed to test hypotheses and our analysis shows that how firms' utilize external source of innovation and enhance their innovation capabilities and achieve global competitiveness.

1. Introduction

The Indian automobile industry has experienced a lot of transformation in the last two decades. With the liberalization and globalization process starting in 1991, the industry has seen the entry of international automobile majors in India. Along with the automobile original equipment manufacturers (OEMs), auto component industry has transformed itself from a traditional job fulfiler role to an integrated organization role (Sahoo, Banwet, and Momaya 2011).The process of technological development in Indian automobile industry can be seen in the auto-clusters. Automobile clusters are developed in North (NCR–Uttaranchal), East (Jamshedpur–Kolkata), South (Chennai–Hosur–Bangalore) and Western (Mumbai–Pune–Aurangabad) regions. Based on technology dynamism, market liberalization and competitiveness, clusters have experienced all the phases of life cycle: pre-foundation phase (1945–1965), emergence phase (1966–1984), growth phase I (1985–1995), growth phase II (1996–2007) and sustenance Phase (year 2008 onwards).

Indian Government has contributed in automobile industry growth by liberalizing the norms for foreign direct investment (FDI) and import of technology in 1990s. As a result, the production of total vehicles increased from 4.2 million in 1998–1999 to 10.7 million in 2011–2012. Due to intense competition and changing customer demand, product development process advances have been more significant than changes in the product architecture. Product cycles continue to grow shorter as more companies adopt the simultaneous engineering approach pioneered by Japanese automakers. The degree of scale economies in the industry is closely associated with the flexibility of the technology to constantly produce different models from the same platform. Some of the major technological issues of current importance are increasing energy efficiency, competency of internal combustion engine, reducing the weight of vehicles, incorporating high-tech safety features, emission norms, etc. (Nag, Banerjee, and Chatterjee 2007). Simultaneously, with the gradual opening up of the auto-component sector, government is extending support for the development of domestic critical component and sub-system suppliers through improvement in the investment environment, stronger patent regimes and incentives for R&D.

In management literature, more recent perspectives, i.e. innovation systems and global value chain perspectives, have highlighted the importance of the dual structure of internal change-generating innovative resources and links to external sources of technology. The innovation systems perspective based on the assumption that technological learning and innovation not only includes economic transactions, but also includes interactive processes involving actors, institutions and social norms (Nelson 1993; Lundvall 1992). The innovation systems perspective (refers to the national, regional or local level) emphasizes the crucial role of technological trajectories and institutional assets in collective learning, giving a special importance to the environment that stimulates technological learning and innovation. Therefore, the organizational and cultural proximity of agents are crucial in local capacity building. The global value chain perspective focuses on the analysis of international linkages among firms in worldwide production and distribution systems, emphasizing the role of leading companies that carry out functional integration and coordinate international dispersed activities (Giuliani, Pietrobelli, and Rabelloti 2005). Global chains operate in highly competitive global markets, fostering the need of multinational corporations/transnational corporations (MNCs/TNCs) to transfer technical and managerial capacities to their local affiliates and suppliers, so that these firms will be able to fulfil the quality standards and lower their production costs. These perspectives have recently been seen as important for understanding the technological dynamics of late industrialization in India.

The aim of this research is to probe innovation systems perspective and global value chain perspective to develop research framework to build innovation capabilities among auto-component manufacturing industry. Based on this framework, our research investigated Indian-Pune automobile cluster and evaluated innovation performance of firms within the cluster and find competitiveness of the cluster firms. Our findings have the following contributions. First, we highlight interaction of macro and micro environments of cluster and explored that effective utilization of external source of innovation and knowledge spillover has strong interrelatedness to build innovation capabilities of firms. Second, among all innovation capabilities, technological, manufacturing and organizational capabilities are most positively related to innovative performance of firms within cluster.

The paper is structured as follows. Section 2 covers review of literature on significance of cluster development and innovations leading to competitiveness. How inter-firm linkages within cluster positively support to create innovative resources and innovation capability fostering small and medium enterprises (SMEs) development and evaluate changing perspectives in prominent segment of India – automobile industry. In Section 3, the conceptual research framework is developed as a determinant of innovation and competitiveness in Pune automobile cluster. Section 4 explores link between externalities at cluster level with firm innovation system and develops research framework and hypotheses. The research methodology, sample selection and data collection procedure are also given in this section. Finally, result validates the research framework and defines the scope for future work.

2. Review of literature

Porter (2003) observed that technology is among the most prominent factors that determine the rules of competition at clusters. Technology and innovations have influenced cluster development process in developing countries. The cluster development process follows cluster life cycle. Cluster development process studied by Menzel (2007) found that dynamism plays an important role between growth and sustenance phases of cluster life cycle. This dynamism mostly happens due to heterogeneity of knowledge and technological and innovation capabilities of firms within cluster. Technological capabilities are uneven within a same cluster, which is largely due to differences in the firms' ability to bring about technological paradigm and trajectory shifts (Narayanan 1998). So, the competence of cluster depends on the level of accumulated technological capability through learning relationships, inter-firm linkages, in-house R&D efforts and innovation capabilities.

2.1 *Cluster inter-firm linkages, innovation capability and SMEs development*

Innovation capability of firm is identified as one of the major factors for the enhancement of performance of firm (Deshpande, Farley, and Webster 1993; Edwards and Delbridge 2001; Yam et al. 2004). Normally, these capabilities of firm are focused on product and process innovations, which may be incremental or radical. The meaning and impact of these innovations changes based on the type of firm. So, firms within cluster are need to possess technological and innovation capabilities. It is unlikely to find all these capabilities in the same firm and they do not innovate in isolation by focusing on in-house R&D, but involves other firms as a part of innovation process. Thus, literature highlights functional, process and strategic approach to accommodate capabilities. The relationship between innovation and firm performance has been explored in many studies as shown in Table 1.

Table 1 explains various capability factors contributing to the performance of firm. Kumaraswamy et al. (2012) studied Indian domestic supplier firms development, as market liberalization progresses, through catch-up strategies aimed at integrating with the industry's global value chain. They found that for continued performance, domestic supplier firms need to adapt their strategies from catching up initially through technology licensing/collaborations and joint ventures with multinational enterprises (MNEs) to developing strong customer relationships with downstream firms. Further, these two strategies lay the foundation for a strategy of knowledge creation through R&D during the integration of domestic industry with the global value chain.

Technology acquisition in developing countries can be related to three major resources, for instance, basic or innovative research through in-house R&D efforts; arm-length purchase of design and drawings through payments of royalty or fees; and import of capital goods with embodied technology (Narayanan and Bhat 2009). Hence, ability of these firms to innovate depends on access to external sources of innovations as well. Acquiring knowledge and skills through external collaboration has become an effective and efficient way towards the success of innovation within clusters (Okada 2004). In Indian automobile industry, joint ventures and technical collaboration played vital role as a source of innovation for local auto-component supplier firms (Okada and Siddharthan 2007).

2.2 *Indian automobile and auto component Industry*

Indian automobile industry comprises of the auto and the auto-component industries. The automobile industry in India has witnessed changing technological landscape in the global automotive industry (Narayanan 1998) and working in terms of the dynamics of an open market (Sahoo,

Table 1. Study approaches and major factors in assessing technological and innovation capabilities.

Study approach	Technological and innovation capability factors	Proposed by
Functional approach	• Investment capability	Lall (1992)
	• Production capability • R&D capability • Learning capability • Resource availability and allocation capability • Manufacturing capability • Marketing capability	Narayanan (1998, 2001) Yam et al. (2004)
Process approach	• Concept generation capability	Lall (1992)
	• Process innovation capability	Chiesa, Coughlan, and Voss (1996)
	• Product development capability • Technology acquisition capability • Catch-up strategy: technology license/collaboration, customer relationship and knowledge creation • Capability in effective use of system, processes and tools • Linkage and network capability	Narayanan (1998) Guo and Guo (2011) Sudhir Kumar and BalaSubrhmanya (2010) Kumaraswamy et al. (2012)
Strategic approach	• Organizational capability	Chiesa, Coughlan, and Voss (1996)
	• Strategic planning and execution capability	Burgelman, Maidique, and Wheelwright (2004)
	• Understanding competitor innovative strategy and market • Structural and cultural affecting internal innovative activities • Leadership capability	Yam et al. (2011)

Source: Extracted from respective literature articles.

Banwet, and Momaya 2011). India is currently world's second largest market for two wheelers, ninth in passenger cars and eighth in commercial vehicle production globally. Many joint ventures, FDI flows, global OEM presence, technological collaborations and supplier development strategy transformed this industry in last one decade. As per the Automotive Mission Plan (2006), the turnover of the industry is expected to increase to USD 145 billion by 2016 and exports are expected to touch USD 35 billion by that time with better choice in design. The increased production and capacity creation in the automobile sector specifically passenger cars and local transportation vehicles is going to accelerate the continuous growth of the auto component industry.

The principle feature of the Indian auto component industry is that it is a high-investment sector of the economy with state-of-the-art technology, and serving a large number of vehicle models. There are over 450 key players in the auto component sector with a total turnover of USD 43.5 billion in 2011–2012. The Indian auto component industry produces a comprehensive range of components, which include engine parts, drive transmission and steering parts, suspension and braking parts, electrical parts, equipment and other parts. Over the years, the industry is successfully working on the path to fulfil its mandate of localization and moving towards being global suppliers. As per ACMA statistics, the auto component exports has risen from USD 760 million in 2002–2003 to USD 6.8 billion in 2011–2012, amounting to 19% of total output. In India, technology acquisition from developed nation through collaborations and alliances has been one of the preferred routes to build capabilities (Narayanan 1998). However, Indian auto and auto-component firms are started gaining strategic technology management capability (Sahoo, Banwet, and Momaya 2011) and focus is shifting towards building own innovation capabilities.

In the rapidly changing global scenario, the concept of attaining competitiveness on the basis of abundant and cheap labour, favorable exchange rates and concessional duty structure is becoming insufficient and therefore, not sustainable. The key questions are: how quickly the industry is able to adapt to the challenges of the fast changing environment and how well the industry is able to integrate the technology management and innovation with the business strategies of the firms. Hence, the main research gaps identified from the literature review are as follows:

(a) In emerging economy like India, different aspects of innovation capabilities like R&D capability, specialized skills for R&D, manufacturing capability, organizational capability, strategic planning and marketing capability of SMEs (auto-component suppliers and subcontractors) have not been studied at automobile cluster.

(b) Sustainable competitiveness of firms within cluster influenced by innovation capability factors has not been studied at Indian automobile cluster context.

3. Determinants of innovation and competitiveness: Pune auto-cluster

In Indian automobile cluster, the leading auto and auto-component firms played the role of technological 'gatekeepers' in clusters and have become source of new knowledge inputs for smaller firms (Okada 2004). Technology support organizations like Automotive Research Association of India (ARAI), Automotive Component Manufacturers of India (ACMA), Society of Indian Automotive Manufacturer (SIAM) and National Automotive Testing and R&D Infrastructure Project are played important roles at the boundary of cluster knowledge-systems with varying degrees of support from local firms.

3.1 *Pune automobile cluster*

Pune has been emerging as a prominent location for the automobile sector and having advantage of large supplier base as well as proximity of the Nhava Sheva port. It is home to the ARAI, which is responsible for the homologation of all vehicles available in India along with automobile R&D, testing and certification organization. ARAI has tied up with TUV Rheinland, a 130-year-old German multinational and one of the world's largest testing, inspection and certification agencies. With this association, the Indian manufacturers will have an edge in exports of vehicles and vehicle parts as all the aspects of testing and certification as per international standards like EEC/ECE will be handled locally by qualified experts. Automobile and related industry in Pune comprises 189 firms. The major products from the Pune cluster are clutch components, gear components, brake components, shafts, axles, valves, engine components, electrical components, etc.

The cluster witnessed technological paradigm shift ranges from New Product launches to the introduction of differentiated products involving updated technology. The increasing strength of such technological capability efforts, knowledge integration and systemic effect (networks) can be major factor to enhance performance of this cluster. For instance, mid-size car segment has high diesel penetration and shift towards diesel driven vehicles in all segments has also contributed to the growth recently. Additionally, Pune cluster has gained strength from the arrival of global OEMs and creating competitiveness through setting up capacities to locally develop and manufacture engines and transmissions with vendor development as a key part of their strategy.

The Auto Cluster Project was set up to support SMEs in design, rapid prototyping, calibration, environment testing and polymer component testing facilities. The manufacturing facilities are largely flexible, where new firms also established a modern shop-floor arrangement which integrates technology for differentiated vehicles. This arrangement enabled the firms to effectively utilize their capacity by changing their product mix and to ensure quality and timely delivery. Also there is change in the use of advanced materials to reduce a vehicle weight and improve fuel and drag efficiency. Global OEMs have established their R&D centres and Pune cluster is gaining outsourcing capabilities in R&D space. These all changes constitute a technological paradigm shifts and firms following various knowledge acquisition channels leading to inter-firm variation.

3.2   *Conceptual research framework*

The conceptual research framework is proposed based on literature review as shown in Figure 1. It enables us to understand auto-component suppliers and subcontractors (SMEs) relationship with global and domestic OEMs (contractor). SMEs deliver products or services to the contractor as specified by their production requirements. Sudhir Kumar and BalaSubrhmanya (2010) explored that subcontracting firms receive assistance from the contractor and the degree of inter-firm linkages between the participating firms has assessed in terms of assistance. He probed the inter-firm linkages and diversity of assistance that SMEs would obtain through subcontracting with TNC in the Indian automobile industry and role of this assistance in their economic performance.

The literature in the Indian context does not show how these types of assistance build innovative resources and innovation capability among SMEs to enhance cluster competitiveness. The entering MNEs possess sophisticated technological and managerial capabilities that domestic incumbents lack. Consequently, domestic firms need to 're-orient' themselves by making changes to their strategies, structures, technologies, systems and organizational practices/routines. The capabilities mostly rest on absorptive capacity and technological learning patterns (Guo and Guo 2011) of local firms within cluster, which reduces the technology gap between domestic and foreign firms, increasing the probability of linkages and spillovers. The availability, competence and geographic proximity of local suppliers also increase the likelihood of local sourcing and inter-firm linkages (Contreras, Carrillo, and Alonso 2012).Our research explores how sources of innovation and knowledge spillover at cluster (macro environment) interact with the innovation capability of firms (micro-level environment) to get enhanced innovation performance of SMEs and improve competitiveness.

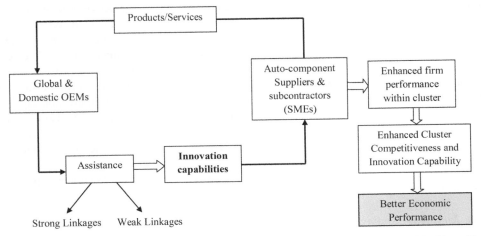

Figure 1.   The conceptual framework for influence of OEMs on innovation capabilities of SMEs and better economic performance.

4. Research framework and methodology

The research framework is developed based on conceptual framework and validated at Indian-Pune automobile cluster.

4.1 *Development of research framework and hypotheses*

4.1.1 *Link between innovation systems and global value chain perspective:*

The innovation systems perspective literature describes the link between innovation and competitive and economic outcomes at the national level (Porter 1998; Nelson 1993). Various studies adopted the RIS approach to examine innovating firms in the context of the generation and diffusion of knowledge among RIS actors that takes place outside the boundary of the firm. The critical factor to build innovation capability of firm within cluster is 'external sources of innovation'. Whereas, the global value chains perspective is concerned with how the dispersal, coordination and re-integration of value chains among group of firms across region governed, how the institutions seek to influence this governance and the regional competitiveness and social standards (Gupta and Subramanian 2008). It also emphasis on learning from external sources is critical in emerging economies to avoid lock-in at low-end of value chain. Thus, it emphasis on knowledge spillovers and collective learning is critical to clusters. Also knowledge spillover has influence on sources of innovation to create 'competitive linkages' and 'collaborative linkages' (Contreras, Carrillo, and Alonso 2012).

Hypothesis H1: Knowledge spillover has positive relationship with external sources of innovation at Pune automobile cluster.

Hypothesis H2: External source of innovation has positive relationship with knowledge spillover at Pune automobile cluster

4.1.2 *External source of innovation*

Earlier studies of source of innovation have focused on firm-specific determinants as in-house R&D activities, manufacturing innovation and firm size. The source of innovation is important because it determines the capabilities a firm that must possess to adopt the necessary innovations in time to achieve success in the marketplace. Studies commented that innovations are not only determined by factors internal to firms, but also determined by an interactive process involving relationships between firms and different actors in the regional innovation system. Firms cannot innovate in isolation but they tend to complement their ability to create knowledge in-house by utilizing knowledge from external sources of innovation. Interaction with external sources of innovation can provide missing external inputs into the learning process that the firm cannot provide itself (Romjin and Albaladejio 2002) and improve firm performance (Caloghirou, Kastelli, and Tsakanika 2004). Hence, firms can reinforce their innovation capability by importing technologies and then diffusing, assimilating, communicating and absorbing them into their organizations (Hamel and Prahalad 1990) and capabilities developed are largely related to its acquisition of knowledge external to the firm and its integration of such knowledge.

Hypothesis H3: External source of innovation has positive relationship with innovation capability factors of firms within cluster.

4.1.3 *Knowledge spillover*

The knowledge spillover plays dual role at cluster level as well as within firm to build innovation capabilities. Knowledge spillover result from dynamism in the information and knowledge flows about products, processes, technologies, consumers and markets, which circulate informally within the system (Figure 2).

Hypothesis H4: Knowledge spillover has positive relationship with innovation capability factors of firms within cluster.

4.1.4 *Relationship between innovation capability and innovation performance*

A firm's competitive advantage could come from the efficiency and capabilities derived from new product developments (Lawless and Fisher 1990). An increase in product and process innovation is attributable to the accumulation of capabilities and contributes to innovation outputs. Improving innovation capabilities can be beneficial to the firm and lead to enhanced competitiveness (Yam et al. 2004). Narayanan (1998) regarded R&D activities as a central component of firms' technological innovation activities in automobile industry and as the most important intangible form of innovation expenditure (Evangelista et al. 1997). The firm's specific competencies contribute substantially to its sales growth and competitive advantage. There is a causal connection between a firm's resources and its technological innovation performance. The OLSO Manual proposed that technological and innovation performance can be measured by the proportion of sales due to technologically new or improved products, i.e. sales performance. This indicator has also been widely adopted in recent innovation studies (Yam et al. 2011).

Hypothesis H5: Innovation capabilities have positive influence on firm's innovative performance within Pune automobile cluster.

These hypotheses tested in Pune automobile cluster and the next section narrates study variables.

4.1.5 *Study variables*

Table 2 covers all variables for this research. Based on the literature review, following major and support variables are defined for study.

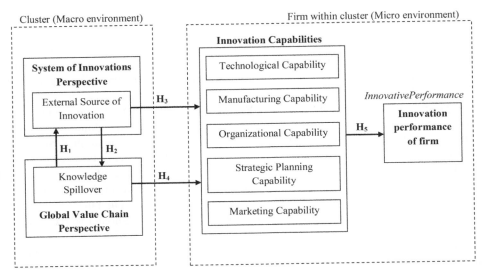

Figure 2. Research framework.

4.2 *Research methodology: sample selection, data collection and analysis*

Empirical qualitative and quantitative research methodology is adopted to test the hypotheses. The empirical evidences are collected from 108 auto-component supplier firms and the primary 341 responses are analysed.

4.2.1 *Sample selection*

The Pune auto and auto-component cluster has been selected for the study and study was carried out from January 2012 to September 2012. This cluster spread in the Pune–Mumbai–Aurangabad belt of Maharashtra state, India and consists 19 auto firms and 170 auto-component supplier firms. Study included interview-based and survey-based methodology, where totally 56 interviews were conducted in three different stages and sample survey of 108 auto-component firms (large Tier I and II, medium Tier I and II and small Tier III firms) was performed.

The first phase was a qualitative study comprising pilot interviews during January 2012–March 2012 with lead auto firms managers, local SMEs owners and engineers. We have understood development of cluster, benchmark dimensions of cluster and their interaction, technological change agents and innovation capability building process in the cluster. Then, we carried out a round of formal interviews during July 2012–September 2012. The experts were chosen as follows: (1) engineers and managers those have worked in the cluster for more than 10 years; (2) they have rich mobility experiences (trainings, trade fairs, members of associations, etc.) within the cluster; (3) local SMEs owners; (4) seven experts were from R&D background and (5) five experts were from ARAI Pune, Auto Cluster Project, Maratha Chamber of Commerce for Industry and Agriculture (MCCIA), United Nations Industrial Development Organization (UNIDO) and University of Pune, respectively. In the second phase of study, we performed a survey on 108 auto-component firms selected from the list of SIAM and ACMA members. We have also collected multiple responses from same firms and computed the averages as the scores used in the analysis to increase the reliability of the data. The total 341 responses were collected from 108 firms in this primary survey. Based on the literature and interaction with experts, we have designed the questionnaire.

4.2.2 *Data collection and measurement:*

The study questionnaire contained three parts. The first part was about basic information, including the firm's year of establishment, number of employees and lines of business, as well as respondents' related information (title, job tenure and years of work experience in the line of business, mobility within cluster). The second part consists of innovative sales performance intensity of firm from last three years. It can be calculated as sum of R&D expenditure, import of components and raw material, expenditure on advertisement and sales promotion, foreign expenditure on technology know how/services, import of capital goods and skill by aales turnover multiplied by 100. The proxy variables are defined and used depending on the type of firm. The size of firm gets normalized due to sales turnover. The third part was about the degree of influence/impact of innovation capabilities on innovative performance of firm within Pune auto-cluster. Also, it covers how firm innovation system interacts with cluster innovation system and global value chain to build innovation capabilities. We have asked respondents to answer the question on the basis of five-point Likert ordinal Scale (1 = very low, 2 = low, 3 = average/moderate, 4 = high and 5 = very high). The variables are measured as percentage coded to ordinal scale of 1, 2, 3, 4 and 5 (from 0 to 20–21, more than 20 and up to 40–42, more than 40 and up to 60–63, more than 60 and up to 80–84 and more than 80 and up to 100–105) to have a consistency with other variables.

Table 2. Details of support variables to evaluate innovation capability and innovative performance of firms within a cluster.

		Variable name
I. Knowledge spillover		
(1)	The ability of knowledge transfer through available scientific base/ publication (codified formal knowledge transfer)	SPILLSCIENCE
(2)	Extent of information and knowledge flows about products, processes, technologies, consumer and markets circulate informally within cluster	SPILLINFORMAL
(3)	Extent of knowledge transfer due to mobilization of peoples within cluster firms	PEOPLEMOBI
(4)	Knowledge spillover through socio-professional and local markets	LOCALSPILL
(5)	The percentage of components/products supplied to specific OEM	SUPPLYCOMP
(6)	Extent of support in terms of technical and managerial capacities from MNCs/ Global OEMs	SPILLMNC
II. External sources of innovations		
(7)	The ability of acquisition of embodied technology	TECHEMBOD
(8)	The extent of patent disclosure/scientific knowledge/participation in trade and exhibitions	PATENT
(9)	The extent of FDI flows/venture funding/other financial support for technology development	FDIFLOW
(10)	The extent of lead users/customer innovations	CUSTOMERINNO
(11)	Extent of strategic technology alliances/international linkages among production and distribution systems	INTLINKAGE
III. Technological capability		
(12)	The ability of in-house R&D/design and development efforts towards product development	RNDPRODUCT
(13)	The ability of in-house R&D/design and development efforts towards production process/engineering development	RNDPROCESS
(14)	The level of R&D/design and development equipment's used	RNDEQUIP
(15)	The extent of technology acquisition efforts like technology purchasing/ alliance/proprietary technology	TECHAQUISITION
(16)	The percentage of specialized skills allocated to R&D/design and development department	RNDSKILLS
(17)	The ability of complex/discrete components being manufactured	COMPLEXCOMP
(18)	The extent to which the auto firms (as contractors) provides detailed specifications and designs of the product	SPECIFICS
(19)	The extent to which contractor/customer provides feedback on product performance and quality for improvement	FEEDBACK
(20)	The extent to which learning patterns/orientation adapted	LEARNING
IV. Manufacturing capability		
(21)	The ability of transforming R&D/design and development output into production	RNDPRODUCTION
(22)	The ability of applying advanced manufacturing methods like JIT,TQM, Six Sigma, Toyota production system, etc./degree of automation	ADVMFGMETHO
(23)	The ability of maintaining flexibility and lead time for shop floor	FLEXILEADTIME
(24)	The ability of effective use of learning curves/experience	LEARNCURVE
(25)	The percentage of skilled workforce at manufacturing	SKILLMFG
(26)	The extent of incremental innovations occurred in process development	INNOVATION
V. Organizational capability		
(27)	The ability of handling multiple R&D/innovation projects parallel	MULTIPROJ
(28)	The extent to which coordination and cooperation between R&D, manufacturing and marketing	COORDICOOPER
(29)	The ability of high-level integration and control on major functions	FUNCCONTORL
(30)	The ability towards developing absorptive capacity and in-house learning	ABSORPTIVE
(31)	The ability of effective implementation of organizational routines towards innovation	ORGROUTINES

(Continued)

Table 2. (Continued)

VI. Marketing capability		
(32)	The ability of relationship management with major customers	CRM
(33)	The ability of time to market new products/reduction of new technology development time from concept to market	TIMETOMARKET
(34)	The extent of good knowledge about different market segments	MARKETSEGM
(35)	The ability of having efficient sales force/marketing programme	
(36)	The ability of excellent after sales services	AFTERSERVICE
VII. Strategic planning capability		
(37)	The ability of identifying strengths and weakness	STRENTHWEAK
(38)	The ability of identifying external opportunity and threats	OPPORTHREAT
(39)	The extent of having clear goals	GOALS
(40)	The ability of having road map of new product and process with measureable milestones	ROADMAP
(41)	The ability of effective resource allocation to all SBU's/STU's	RESOURCES
(42)	The ability of highly adapted and responsive to external environment	EXTENVIRON
(43)	The extent to which technology strategy adapted in the firm	TECHSTRATEGY
(44)	Ability of linking technology strategy with business strategy	TECHLINKBUSI

Note: SBU – strategic business units and STU – strategic technology units.

The auto-component suppliers are classified into cognitive sub-groups like small, medium and large based on the number of employees and generally in Indian automotive industry, there is no size difference between Tier I and Tier II large, medium and small firms, and Tier III firms are small and tiny (Uchikawa and Roy 2010).Understanding research focus of the present study, the Pune automotive cluster can be placed into the cognitive subgroups in the cluster as: large auto-component supplier's subgroup 1 (Tier I and Tier II), medium auto-component supplier's subgroup 2 (Tier I and Tier II) and small auto-component supplier's subgroup 3 (Tier I, Tier II and Tier III). Firm size was used as a control variable in this study. Previous studies have indicated that there could be a positive relationship between firm size and technological innovation performance as size can affect a firm's innovation and performance. This study included data from Tier I, Tier II and Tier III auto-component industries, we controlled for the possibility of industry effects in our analysis by using dummy variables for the type of industry. This approach was taken because firms from auto industries may have differing levels of performance in innovation capability and efficiency.

4.2.3 *Data analysis*

Empirical analysis used a two-stage structural equation model (SEM) to test the theoretical model (Anderson and Gerbing 1982; Kline 1998). In the first stage, we developed a measurement model and performed confirmatory factor analyses (CFAs) to demonstrate the model's psychometric properties of reliability, validity and dimensionality. In the second stage, we tested the hypotheses through covariance structure models. We used the SPSS-AMOS software to estimate structural models and the maximum likelihood (ML) method with robust estimators to estimate the parameters to improve the requirements of normality.

The measurement analysis included assessments of the scale reliability, convergent validity, discriminant validity and uni-dimensionality of the research constructs. Cronbach's alpha was used to assess the scale reliability of each construct in the research model. Cronbach's alpha for every factor was greater than the suggested threshold value of 0.7 for an acceptable level of reliability (Kline 1998). The convergent validity of the research constructs was assessed using exploratory factor analysis (EFA). The EFA results showed that all the constructs had eigen values exceeding 1.0

and that all the factor loadings exceeded 0.3. The convergent validity of the research constructs was therefore confirmed. Discriminant validity and uni-dimensionality were assessed using CFA.

The measurement model constructed for CFA had a relative chi-square value of 2.325 < 3, an incremental fit index (IFI) of 0.946 > 0.9 and a comparative fit index (CFI) of 0.916 > 0.9. The standardized loadings (λ) for all constructs were high ($\lambda > 0.5$) and the corresponding t-values were statistically significant. These results indicated uni-dimensionality among the research constructs. A check of the modification indices for the measurement model conducted during the CFA process revealed no significant cross loadings among the variables ($\lambda > 0.85$), which indicated good discriminant validity (Kline 1998). The scores for valid variable items in each construct were then averaged as a single score to be used in the model analysis.

The hypotheses were tested by way of SEM. SEM enables us to test several multiple regression equations at the same time and is therefore a very useful tool for testing overall model fit with a lower degree of measurement error. In the model analysis, ML estimation and standardized regression weighting were used for interpretation. Multiple indices of fit including IFI, CFI and cmin/df were used to specify the overall model fit. The IFI and CFI values were over 0.9 and that of cmin/df was below 3, indicating a good degree of model fit (Bentler 1990). An Root Mean Square Error of Approximation (RMSEA) value of less than 0.7 indicates an adequate degree of model fit (Bollen 1989). The research hypotheses were tested according to the significance of the t-test result in each path, with parameter estimates being made in the SEM process.

5. Results and discussion

Indian auto industry has confirmed that technical collaborations have not only helped domestic firms to upgrade their technological capabilities, but have also improved their productivity and operational efficiency significantly. Our results demonstrate the empirical evidence collected during the interviews with local suppliers. We identified a pattern in the process of strengthening the technological and manufacturing capabilities through their interaction with leading firms. The inclusion of suppliers in value chain follows stages such as: problem solving, trust building, diversified supplier and outsourcing of engineering, quality control and maintenance. As a result, the local provider becomes fully included in the assembly plant's supply chain and knowledge spillover plays an important role to position supplier firms at global value chain.

Indian components firms such as the TVS Group, the Rane Group, the TACO group and the Kalyani Group have successfully forged strong Tier I relationships with domestic and MNE auto manufacturers and have become integral parts of the auto industry's global supply chain. Indian Tier I firms were very flexible, for instance, they could manufacture components for different auto manufacturers and for different models at very low volumes with fully automated plant. The Tier II firms have begun to develop design competencies to focus on growing export markets. In other words, there is a considerable focus on developing world-class capabilities and using these to move to higher value-added activities. The empirical results performed by SEM comprise descriptive statistics shown in Table 3. A good degree of model fit was observed for proposed model by overall fit of indices. The model yielded cmin/df of 1.259 < 3, CFI of 0.943 > 0.9 and RMSEA of 0.043 < 0.07. The study supports research framework by indicating utilization of external sources of innovation in enhancing innovation capabilities and thus it has influence on innovation performance of firms within cluster. The hypothesis testing revealed that all innovation capabilities can be enhanced by external source of innovation and this will not happen without effective utilization of knowledge spillover. Innovation systems perspective positively interacts with innovation capabilities of firm within cluster.

Pune automobile cluster is still in process of gaining indigenous R&D capability to develop critical components. Technologically innovative products are normally developed by technology acquisition from developed nations and automation at manufacturing processes observed through active assistance in the cluster. Hence, the ability of embodied technology acquisition, patent disclosure/scientific knowledge, strategic technology alliances, knowledge spillover through assistance from domestic and global OEMs and technology transfer are major sources of innovation for Pune automobile cluster. However, effectiveness of the technology and knowledge transfer depends on the competence of people involved and business strategy of the firm (Teece 1996). The success of firm largely based on its effective learning capability and exploiting the available knowledge. Technological capability is construed as an ongoing process of learning and indicating greater attention to in-house R&D capability building. To some extent, mobilization of people and spin-offs specifically from Tata Motors (TELCO then) have played significant role in the region with respect to technology transfer.

It is evident that cluster firms are positioning themselves in global value chain and knowledge spillover can act as bridge enabling the firm to improve the effectiveness of its knowledge transfer activities. Result of hypothesis testing shown in Table 4 and Figure 3. In Figure 3, the unidirectional arrows represent the regression relationship between two variables. Our research contribution shows that firm capability of external sources of innovation utilization builds innovation capability having impact on in-house R&D activities, innovative manufacturing practices and absorptive capability within cluster. Also our findings indicate that knowledge spillover plays dual role. It has become one of the sources of innovation for effective transfer of knowledge and positively related to manufacturing capability as well as technological capability. These capabilities of firm were enhanced by formal and informal knowledge transfer, socio-professional and local markets and technical and managerial support from auto firms. Knowledge spillover has no direct impact on other capabilities of firms. Experts claimed that new problem solving methods have been adapted within cluster due to technology acquisition, strategic technology alliances and support from global OEMs rather than consultancy firm or universities. Hence, both external sources of innovation and knowledge spillover externalities have dominant influence on building innovation capabilities of firm within a cluster.

The SEM results shows that cluster firm's innovation capabilities are enhanced by external sources of innovation and positively related to technological capability, manufacturing capability,

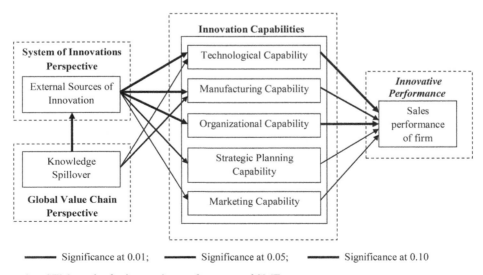

Figure 3. SEM results for innovative performance of SMEs.

Table 3. Descriptive statistics and correlations among study variables.

Variables	Mean	SD	1	2	3	4	5	6	7	8
External sources of innovation	3.435	1.422	1							
Knowledge Spillover	1.947	1.106	0.390**	1						
Technological capability	3.660	1.078	0.220**	0.024**	1					
Manufacturing capability	3.452	1.245	0.315**	0.245**	0.436**	1				
Organizational capability	3.124	1.067	0.347**	0.209**	0.505**	0.618**	1			
Strategic planning capability	3.507	1.128	0.259**	0.113*	0.432**	0.721**	0.624**	1		
Marketing capability	3.744	1.023	0.172*	0.082	0.484**	0.556**	0.549**	0.483**	1	
Innovative sales performance	1.896	1.547	0.132[+]	0.168*	0.081	0.302**	0.310**	0.346**	0.150*	1

$**p < 0.01.$
$*p < 0.05.$
$^{+}p < 0.1.$

organizational capability, marketing capability and strategic planning capability. Most importantly, learning capability has positive effect to build technological capability and influence innovative performance of firms. Cohen and Levinthal (1990) supports our finding that an organizational unit's internal learning capability determines the extent to which it can absorb new knowledge from other units.

Among all innovation capabilities, technological capability (includes in-house R&D, learning and R&D resource allocation capability), manufacturing and organizational capability are most positively related to innovative performance (sales performance) of firm's within Pune automobile cluster. As sales performance measured the percentage of sales generated by technologically new or improved products in last three years, it concerned not only the design and manufacture of new or improved products, but also the production of new or improved products that are marketable. Yam et al. (2011) have measured technological innovation performance of Hong Kong manufacturing industries. This study adapted similar approach to measure innovation performance of firm in terms of sales performance.

The covariance between capability variables has been tested by the CFA and results are shown in the appendix. The measurement model constructed for CFA had a relative chi-square value of $2.325 < 3$, an IFI of $0.946 > 0.9$ and a CFI of $0.916 > 0.9$. The standardized loadings (λ) for all constructs were high ($\lambda > 0.5$) and the corresponding t-values were statistically significant. These results indicated uni-dimensionality among the research constructs and the measurement model conducted during the CFA process revealed no significant cross-loadings among the variables ($\lambda > 0.85$), which indicated good discriminant validity (Kline 1998). Thus, capability variables are not highly correlated. The result also shows that technological capability, i.e. in-house R&D capability and organizational capability, counts more than marketing and strategic planning capability to enhance innovative firm performance.

Innovative performance of firm's within cluster enhanced mainly due to in-house R&D efforts towards product and production process development, extent of technology acquisition, specialized skills and learning orientations. Interestingly, large auto-component firms are building ability of manufacturing complex or discrete components and getting active support in product development in few cases. Manufacturing capability has positive effect on the performance because of

Table 4. Hypothesis testing and SEM results.

Hypothesized paths	Regression estimate	Standardized regression estimate (r)	Critical ratio	Hypothesis supported
H1: Knowledge Spillover → External sources of innovation(ESI)	0.175	0.156***	3.882	Yes
H2: External sources of innovation →Knowledge spillover (KS)	0.064	0.060	1.453	No
H3-a: ESI → Technological capability	0.127	0.147***	3.355	Yes
H3-b: ESI → Manufacturing capability	0.217	0.223***	5.336	Yes
H3-c: ESI →Organizational Capability	0.282	0.391***	10.026	Yes
H3-d: ESI → Strategic Planning Capability	0.560	0.362**	9.164	Yes
H3-e: ESI → Marketing capability	0.432	0.452*	10.750	Yes
H4-a: KS → Technological capability	0.287	0.239**	5.802	Yes
H4-b: KS → Manufacturing capability	0.173	0.134**	4.396	Yes
H4-c: KS→Organizational Capability	−0.044	−0.056	1.336	No
H4-d: KS→ Strategic Planning Capability	0.038	0.062	1.572	No
H4-e: KS→ Marketing capability	−0.042	−0.070	1.724	No
H5-a: Technological Capability → innovative performance of firm	0.166	0.263***	6.637	Yes
H5-b: Manufacturing Capability → innovative performance of firm	0.152	0.112**	2.797	Yes
H5-c: Organizational Capability → innovative performance of firm	0.132	0.235***	5.781	Yes
H5-d: Strategic planning Capability → innovative performance of firm	0.482	0.688*	3.691	Yes
H5-e: Marketing Capability → innovative performance of firm	0.367	0.574*	4.228	Yes
Control Variables				
Size →innovation firm performance	−0.035	−0.044	−1.044	
Age →innovation firm performance	−0.057	−0.046	−1.344	
Goodness of fit indexes				
Cmin/df	1.259	Less than 3		
CFI	0.943	Greater than 0.9		
IFI	0.958	Greater than 0.9		
RMSEA	0.043	Less than 0.07		

***$p < 0.01$.
**$p < 0.05$.
*$p < 0.10$.

ability of applying advanced manufacturing methods (mostly defined by OEMs), ability to maintain flexibility and lead time at shop floor, effective use of learning/experience curves and incremental innovations. Organization capability also played decisive role in enhancing innovative performance by developing ability of firm transforming R&D and design output into production and extent of coordination among departments like manufacturing, marketing and R&D within organization. Large auto-component firms are engaged into developing organizational routines for innovation and better absorptive capacity development. Moreover, experts asserted that overall sales performance of firm has an impact of marketing but our hypothesis testing result of innovative performance of firm has not strongly supported this argument. This is mainly because, automobile OEMs are more focused on performance characteristics of auto-components and timely delivery.

6. Conclusion

This research has contributed towards both theoretical and practical aspects. The growing attention of global value chain perspective and innovation systems perspective has been accounted. Their interaction with firm innovation capability within a cluster proves that effective utilization of external sources of innovation and knowledge spillover has strong interconnectedness to build innovation capability as well as provide competitive advantage. The outcome of research confirms dual role of knowledge spillover as a source of innovation for effective knowledge transfer and its influence on technological and manufacturing capability. Also, it highlights the positive interaction between regional innovation system and firm innovation system. Our empirical results have shown that external sources of innovation have positively related to enhance all innovation capabilities of firms within a cluster. Moreover, it demonstrates that technological capability (includes in-house R&D, learning and R&D resource allocation capability), manufacturing and organizational capability are most positively related to the innovative performance of firm's within Pune automobile cluster. Thus, industry leaders can develop needed innovation ecosystem based on these insights to enhance the performance and become global players. The bigger sample size and cross-cluster data may produce more statistically accurate results in the model testing process. The future research direction may consider comparative study between various clusters from different geographic locations as well as different sectors.

Acknowledgements

Authors would like to thank reviewers for their useful and insightful comments which helped us to enrich this paper. We would also like to thank all managers and executives for their views and contribution to this research by filling survey questionnaire. Finally, we are thankful to Knowledge Forum too.

References

Anderson, J. C., and D. W. Gerbing. 1982. "Some Methods for Re-specifying Measurement Models to Obtain Uni-dimensional Constructs Measures." *Journal of Marketing Research* 19 (4): 453–460.

Bentler, P. M. 1990. "Comparative Fit Indexes in Structural Models." *Psychological Bulletin* 107 (2): 238–246.

Bollen, K. A. 1989. *Structural Equations with Latent Variables*. New York: Wiley.

Burgelman, R., M. A. Maidique, and S. C. Wheelwright. 2004. *Strategic Management of Technology and Innovation*. New York: McGraw Hill.

Caloghirou, Y., I. Kastelli, and A. Tsakanika. 2004. "Internal Capabilities and External Knowledge Sources: Complements or Substitutes for Innovative Perfromance?" *Technovation* 24 (1): 29–39.

Chiesa, V., P. Coughlan, and C. A. Voss. 1996. "Development of Technical Innovation Audit." *Journal of Product Innovation Management* 13 (2): 105–136.

Cohen, W. M., and F. A. Levinthal. 1990. "Absorptive Capacity a New Perspective on Learning and Innovation." *Administrative Science Quarterly* 35 (1): 128–152.

Contreras, F., J. Carrillo, and J. Alonso. 2012. "Local Entrepreneurship within Global Value Chains: A Case Study in the Mexican Automotive Industry." *World Development* 40 (5): 1013–1023.

Deshpande, R., J. U. Farley, and F. E. Webster. 1993. "Corporate Culture, Customer Orientation, and Innovativeness in Japanese Firms: AQuadrat Analysis." *Journal of Marketing* 57 (1): 23–37.

Edwards, T., and R. Delbridge. 2001. "Linking Innovation Potential to SME Performance: An Assessment of Enterprises in Industrial South Wales." Paper for 41st European regional science association meeting, Zagreb, Croatia.

Evangelista, R., G. Perani, F. Raptit, and D. Archibugi. 1997. "Nature and Impact of Innovation in Manufacturing: Some Evidences from the Italian Innovation Survey." *Research Policy* 26 (4–5): 521–536.

Giuliani, E., C. Pietrobelli, and R. Rabelloti. 2005. "Upgrading in Global Value Chains: Lessons from Latin American Clusters." *World Development* 33 (4): 549–573.

Guo, B., and J. Guo. 2011. "Patterns of Technological Learning within the Knowledge Systems of Industrial Clusters in Emerging Economies: Evidence from China." *Technovation* 31 (2–3): 87–104.

Gupta, V., and R. Subramanian. 2008. "Seven Perspectives on Regional Clusters and the Case of Grand Rapids Office Furniture City." *International Business Review* 17 (4): 371–384.

Hamel, G., and C. K. Prahalad. 1990. "The Core Competence of the Corporation." *Harvard Business Review* 68 (3): 71–91.

Kline, R. B. 1998. *Principles and Practice of Structural Equation Modeling*. New York: The Guilford Press.

Kumaraswamy, A., R. Mudambi, H. Saranga, and A. Tripathy. 2012. "Catch-up Strategies in the Indian Auto Component Industry: Domestic Firms' Responses to Market Liberalization." *Journal of International Business Studies* 43 (4): 368–395.

Lall, S. 1992. "Technological Capabilities and Industrialization." *World Development* 20 (2): 165–186.

Lawless, M. J., and R. J. Fisher. 1990. "Sources of Durable Competitive Advantages in New Products." *Journal of Product Innovation Management* 7 (1): 35–43.

Lundvall, B. 1992. National System of Innovation: Towards a Theory of Innovation and Interactive Learning.

Lorentzen, J. 2005. "The Absorptive Capacities of South African Automotive Component Suppliers." *World Development* 33 (7): 1153–1182.

Menzel, M.-P. 2007. "Networks and Technologies in an Emerging Cluster: The Case of Bioinstruments in Jena." In *Industrial Clusters and Inter-firm Networks*, edited by C. Karlsson, B. Johansson and R. R. Stough, 413–449. Cheltenham: Edward Elgar.

Nag, B., S. Banerjee, and R. Chatterjee. 2007. "Changing Features of the Automobile Industry in Asia: Comparison of Production, Trade and Market Structures in Selected Countries." Asia-Pacific Research and Training Network on Trade, Working paper series No. 37.

Narayanan, K. 1998. "Technology Acquisition, De-regulation and Competitiveness: A Study of Indian Automobile Industry." *Research Policy* 27 (2): 215–228.

Narayanan, K. 2001. "Liberalization and Differential Conduct and Performance of Firms: A Study of Indian Automobile Sector." Discussion Paper Series a No.414, the Institute of Economic research, Hitotsubashi University and United Nations University Institute of Advanced Studies.

Narayanan, K., and S. Bhat. 2009. "Technology Sourcing and its Determinants: A Study of Basic Chemical Industry in India." *Technovation* 29 (8): 562–573.

Nelson, R. R. 1993. *National Innovation Systems: A Comparative Analysis*. New York: Oxford University Press.

Okada, A. 2004. "Skills Development and Inter-firm Learning Linkages under Globalization: Lessons from Indian Automobile Industry." *World Development* 32 (7): 1265–1288.

Okada, A., and N. S. Siddharthan. 2007. "Industrial Clusters in India: Evidence from Automobile Clusters in Chennai and the National Capital Region." Discussion paper no. 103, Institute of Developing Economies, JETRO.

Porter, M. E. 1998. "Clusters and the New Economics of Competition." *Harvard Business Review* 76 (6): 77–90.

Porter, M. E. 2003. "The Economic Performance of Regions." *Regional Studies* 37 (6–7): 549–578.

Romjin, H., and M. Albaladejio. 2002. "Determinants of Innovation Capability in Small Electronics and Software Firms in Southeast England." *Research Policy* 31 (7): 1053–1067.

Sahoo, T., D. K. Banwet, and K. Momaya. 2011. "The Strategic Technology Management in the Auto Component Industry in India." *Journal of Advances in Management Research* 8 (1): 9–29.

Sudhir Kumar, R., and M. H. BalaSubrhmanya. 2010. "Influence of Subcontracting on Innovation and Economic Performance of SMEs in Indian Automobile Industry." *Technovation* 30 (11–12): 558–569.

Teece, D. J. 1996. "Firm Organization, Industrial Structure and Technological Innovation." *Journal of Economic Behavior and Organization* 31 (2): 193–224.

Uchikawa, S., and Roy, S. 2010. "The Development of Auto Component Industry in India." http://ihdindia.org/Formal-and-Informal-Employment/Paper-6-The-Development-of-Auto-Component-Industry-in-India.pdf

Yam, C. M., J. C. Guan, K. F. Pun, and P. Y. Tang. 2004. "An Audit of Technological Capabilities in Chinese Firms: Some Empirical Findings in Beijing China." *Research Policy* 33 (8): 1123–1250.

Yam, C. M., W. Lo, P. Y. Tang, and K. W. Lau. 2011. "Analysis of Sources of Innovation, Technological Innovation Capabilities and Performance: An Empirical study of Hong Kong manufacturing industries." *Research Policy* 40 (3): 391–402.

Appendix

Table A1. Results of CFA.

	Standardized loading (λ)	Error term	t-value
External sources of innovation			
TECHEMBOD	0.78		
PATENT	0.74	0.12	10.12
FDIFLOW	0.89	0.09	9.42
CUSTOMERINNO	0.82	0.16	12.48
INTLINKAGE	0.83	0.07	11.44
Knowledge spillover			
SPILLSCIENCE	0.71		
SPILLINFORMAL	0.83	0.09	10.38
PEOPLEMOBI	0.87	0.11	10.60
LOCALSPILL	0.68	0.17	13.24
SUPPLYCOMP	0.82	0.13	9.55
SPILLMNC	0.72	0.14	12.11
Technological capability			
RNDPRODUCT	0.72		
RNDPROCESS	0.79	0.07	11.42
RNDEQUIP	0.73	0.11	14.88
TECHAQUISITION	0.82	0.09	12.23
RNDSKILLS	0.78	0.10	9.56
COMPLEXCOMP	0.65	0.13	11.78
SPECIFICS	0.86	0.08	8.89
FEEDBACK	0.84	0.09	9.75
LEARNING	0.83	0.10	10.61
Manufacturing capability			
RNDPRODUCTION	0.88		
ADVMFGMETHO	0.76	0.08	12.02
FLEXILEADTIME	0.79	0.07	10.34
LEARNCURVE	0.68	0.07	12.59
SKILLMFG	0.72	0.12	13.33
INNOVATION	0.66	0.18	11.45
Organizational capability			
MULTIPROJ	0.77		
COORDICOOPER	0.64	0.08	12.73
FUNCCONTORL	0.70	0.10	11.62
ABSORPTIVE	0.83	0.07	9.88
ORGROUTINES	0.71	0.12	10.39
Strategic planning capability			
STRENTHWEAK	0.81		
OPPORTHREAT	0.80	0.13	12.73
GOALS	0.81	0.12	10.12
ROADMAP	0.74	0.22	13.90
RESOURCES	0.77	0.17	12.62
EXTENVIRON	0.72	0.12	11.24
TECHSTRATEGY	0.69	0.14	10.77
TECHLINKBUSI	0.70	0.13	11.68
Marketing capability			
CRM	0.79		
TIMETOMARKET	0.67	0.09	12.52
MARKETSEGM	0.76	0.12	10.78
SALESFORCE	0.83	0.11	9.35
AFTERSERVICE	0.71	0.15	11.28

All *t* values are statistically significant.

Influence of outward-foreign direct investment and technological efforts on exports: Indian auto component firms

Neelam Singh

Economics Department, Lady Shri Ram College, Delhi University, Delhi, India

The Indian automotive industry is a classic example of increasing export competitiveness and of emerging market multinationals. Employing a sample of auto component producer–exporters during 2010–2011, we examine the firm-level determinants of the 'Level' at which the firm exports – i.e. the probability of being exporter to original equipment manufacturers (OEMs), and to 'OEMs/Tier firms'. The factors affecting the total value of exports (including aftermarket exports) are also investigated. We analyse the effects of recent outward foreign direct investment (OFDI) – its intensity, and number of manufacturing-OFDI and of non-manufacturing OFDI enterprises – on these dimensions of exports from Home by the firm. We thereby extend the 'substitutability vs. complementarity' hypothesis to the exports 'Level'. The role of technological and marketing variables like ISO14001 is also assessed. While an increase in OFDI intensity consistently increases the total exports, the empirical evidence on the exports 'Level' reflects 'substitutability' in case of intense OFDI-internationalization.

1. Introduction

With a rapid expansion of trade in intermediates – both components and assemblies – in the 1990s and 2000s, the emerging pattern of global trade is marked by a shift from 'trade in goods' to 'trade in value added' and 'trade in tasks' (Gereffi and Lee 2012, 25). Many developing country governments have been attempting to integrate their national firms into the regional/global value chains. The skill and technology intensity of exports and the value-capturing deserve policy emphasis as a country aspires to advance into higher stages of industrialization.

The 2000s, especially the first half, witnessed considerable cross-border foreign direct investment (FDI) flows from emerging economies. At present (2011 figures), the developing nations are a source of over one-fifth of outward foreign direct investment (OFDI) flows.[1] This phenomenon, in turn, has raised several concerns, e.g. the export ramifications for the home developing countries. However, the evidence is sparse.

Highlighting the role of OFDI, this empirical study analyses the firm-level determinants of export competitiveness for a sample of auto component producer–exporters in India. Besides the total exports, we investigate the export participation 'Levels' (status), i.e. being an exporter to original equipment manufacturers (OEMs), and to 'OEMs and/or Tier-firms'. As anticipated, the influence of firm-specific characteristics varies across these aspects of exports. Thus, the policies appropriate for strengthening OEM and high Tier-Level export linkages may somewhat differ from those promoting exports in general. This analysis is also relevant to the global value chain literature.

We examine the impact of intensity of OFDI by the firm in recent years, as the 'substitutability vs. complementarity' hypothesis. Additionally, we distinguish between the influence of manufacturing and non-manufacturing OFDI enterprises. Our findings add to the limited evidence for emerging economies. While examining the effects of technological as well as marketing competencies and efforts, we also investigate the role of international management standards and product certifications, not extensively evaluated so far.

The paper is organized as follows. As the OFDI is a focus explanatory variable, Section 2 reviews the OFDI-exports relationship literature. Section 3 deals with the methodology. Section 4 discusses the sample, data and variables, along with the industry output, exports and OFDI in recent years. Section 5 compares the OFDI-undertaking and other firms in terms of select characteristics. Section 6 presents the estimated models and their analysis. Section 7 concludes the paper.

2. OFDI and exports: review of literature

The early literature on multinational firms posited the question as 'exports vs. OFDI (vs. technology licencing)' choice in the context of horizontal greenfield manufacturing-OFDI by a North-based single-product firm in a two-country framework. The 'substitutability vs. complementarity of exports and OFDI' hypothesis has since been debated and tested (Fonseca, Mendonça, and Passos 2010; Neary 2009; Pradhan 2007).

2.1 Theoretical reasoning

For serving an overseas market, the horizontal manufacturing-OFDI by a firm can substitute its 'potential' exports from the home country (constrained by barriers).[2] However, the OFDI may (i) shift outward the foreign demand curve for the firm's product due to better adaptation to local preferences, and supply and after-sales services reliability, and (ii) reduce unit costs and price, i.e. moving along the curve (Head and Ries 2001; Lipsey and Weiss 1984; Svensson 1996). The affiliate may import intermediates from Home, though may reduce this dependence over time with increasing familiarity with the host country sources. An upstream vertical OFDI can improve the Home operations' export competitiveness. Hence, the net effect of manufacturing-OFDI on exports by the parent firm may arguably go either way. Further this relationship is dynamic (Egger 2001).

For the 'OFDI-exports from Home' analysis, a few more observations are pertinent. First, the OFDI-affiliate's trade with the third countries is relevant – e.g. its sources of intermediates imports and whether it is an export-platform OFDI in a preferential trade agreement area. Second, the aggregation level matters. Subsequent to horizontal manufacturing-OFDI by a firm, any offsetting of 'displaced same product exports' by intermediates exports would be greater for the home economy/industry/business group (having related businesses) than for the investing firm's own (standalone) exports. At firm-level, greater vertical integration generates more counter-balancing (Head and Ries 2001); again, the investing firm may be producing complementary final products, having export potential (Blonigen 2001; Lipsey and Weiss 1984).

Third, the OFDI may reinforce other modes of technology acquisition, like in-house R&D, inward-FDI and tech-import. The South-to-North OFDI seeks exposure to high-income demand patterns, strategic assets and proximity to technology-networks. The reverse knowledge flows (affiliate-to-parent) enhance the export competitiveness of Home operations of emerging multinational enterprises. Cross-border acquisitions offer additionally synergistic knowledge flows and access to acquired brands, marketing networks and established customer-base. For Indian automotive firms Pradhan and Singh (2009) find a favourable effect of greenfield-OFDI on the domestic in-house R&D intensity, comparatively more so of the developed-region OFDI.

2.2 *Empirical evidence*

While the estimated effect of OFDI on exports from the home country has been predominantly positive, the firm-level studies reviewed below, point to more mixed patterns. Pradhan (2007)'s Tobit estimates indicate in general that the OFDI stock to net worth ratio increases the export intensity of Indian manufacturing companies. Narayanan and Bhat (2010) find a strong positive effect of OFDI (dummy) on the export intensity of IT firms in India.

Lipsey and Weiss (1984) analyse for 15 US industries the firm-level total exports from Home to five developed areas. They find generally a significant positive effect of the firm's manufacturing affiliates sales in that area (net of imports from Home). For Japanese manufacturer-exporters, Head and Ries (2001) explain the log-exports in terms of log of (one-year lagged) number of manufacturing and distribution-OFDI 'new investments'. For the overall sample, the effect of distribution-OFDI and for highly integrated firms, also that of manufacturing-OFDI is favourable and significant. In separate estimates for auto *Keiretsu*-members, for the auto-parts suppliers both their own and the Leaders' (vehicle producers') manufacturing OFDI-counts have significant positive influence, while the own distribution-OFDI is unimportant. For Swedish MNCs, Svensson (1996) finds the net effect of foreign production for local sales (reduced form Tobit estimates) on exports from Home by the parent firm to be insignificant, but significant negative in case of particularly export-oriented affiliates.

Swedenborg (2001) analyses the effect of net value of foreign production on Swedish MNCs total exports from Home, and finds it significant and positive in two-stage least-squares equations without firm dummies but highly insignificant in equations including these dummies. Considering the foreign production endogeneity, she used 'age of the firm's oldest manufacturing-OFDI affiliate in the host country' as an instrument-variable. B. A. Blonigen – in his 'Comments' on this study (pp. 131–134) – points to the likelihood of its correlation with the export-equation error term, and the OFDI-exports relationship having a life-cycle and structural breaks.

3. Methodology

Before discussing the relationships being examined by us, a few remarks regarding the automotive industry are in order. Several studies – e.g. Pradhan and Singh (2009); Singh (2010) – discuss the catching-up by Indian automotive firms and the government policies. Learning through exports, integrating into industry global/regional value chains and exporting directly to multinational enterprises (MNEs) are part of this journey. India's share in global exports of auto components has been growing and in 2011 it was 0.7% (ACMA 2012, 14).

In the automotive industry component producers selling directly to vehicle manufacturers are called direct suppliers to OEMs or Tier-1 suppliers.[3] Those selling to Tier-1 suppliers are called Tier-2 suppliers, and so on for lower Tier-(3 and 4) suppliers. There is a huge replacement/aftermarket for auto components used for repair of vehicles. As intermediates for vehicle production, auto components may be supplied as parts or as modules/sub-modules, called assemblies/sub-assemblies.

The cost-competitiveness usually plays a decisive role for pure aftermarket and Low-Tier supplies. However, export supplies to OEMs and high-Tier firms are likely to require: relatively superior engineering, technological, quality and delivery capabilities; greater product complexity and modularisation; and product (vehicle)-recall associated and other risk-taking abilities (Singh 2010). In-house R&D and testing facilities enable quicker designing and modification of critical components as per the OEM's specification. These supply linkages offer several benefits, namely relatively high value added, large contracts and much mutual learning.

Employing a sample of producer–exporters, we explain the determinants of the highest 'Level' of export participation: (a) being exporter to OEMs (XerO) and (b) being exporter to 'OEMs and/or Tier-firms' (XerOT) rather than exporting only for purely aftermarket supplies. In other words, we examine the status of the exporter. Logistic regressions are obtained for the binary variables XerO and XerOT; the respective export values are unavailable. We examine additionally the (log) value of total exports, ExportsL. We have not come across any empirical analysis of exports-participation 'Level', as elaborated above, except by Singh (2010) for auto component firms in India during 2004–2005. Our study for a recent year 2010–2011 combines data from several sources, and investigates the effects of OFDI as a focus explanatory characteristic and of several indicators of technological and commercial capabilities and efforts.

3.1 *OFDI*

For Indian auto component firms, OFDI has become a perceptible phenomenon since around mid-2000s. Still at firm-level the OFDI flows are generally sporadic. We employ data on cumulative OFDI by the firm during July 2007 to March 2012. The equity outflows are considered, except in a few preliminary equations by defining OFDI inclusive of loans and guarantees issued. We analyse the role of equity-OFDI intensity, measured as ratio to sales (*OFDIEint*), or alternatively as ratio to total assets (*OFDIE_Asset*) of the investing firm. While factors like productivity would have a bearing on the sales, there is historical valuation of total assets. Incidentally, both measures being highly correlated for our sample, yield similar results, as seen later. We also estimate the separate effects of number of manufacturing and non-manufacturing OFDI enterprises (*OFDInoE_Mfg, OFDInoE_~Mfg*). A few equations estimate instead the effect of total number of OFDI countries, *OFDInoC* indicating the OFDI-spread.

	Expected sign in equation		
↓ Variable: OFDI	XerO	XerOT	ExportsL
•Intensity, *OFDIEint* or *OFDIE_Asset*	+	+	+
•Intensity square	–	–	–
•Manufacturing enterprises (No.), *OFDInoE_Mfg*	–	–	?
•Non-manufacturing enterprises (No.), *OFDInoE_~Mfg*	+	+	+

Relatively low levels of OFDI intensity may cater to marketing and simple assembly operations; a more OFDI-intensive firm may initiate foreign manufacturing (Svensson 1996). The OFDI intensity is expected to have a tapering-off effect on total exports, while for OEM or up to Tier-Level exporter status (XerO and XerOT) explained variables, the relationship can turn inverse U-shaped – changing from complementarity to substitutability.

The trade-supporting OFDI affiliates can act as resellers/conduit for host country sales of goods exported from Home to the affiliate and facilitate quick delivery. The local exposure and networking through these affiliates may also increase the probabilities of having OEM or up to Tier-Level exports from Home (XerO and XerOT). Vehicle OEMs and Tier-1 firms usually prefer to buy modules and sub-modules. A manufacturing-OFDI affiliate having the requisite manufacturing facilities and competencies may supply to such customers in the host nation and its neighbouring areas, partly replacing the investor firm's similar exports from Home. In India, many large auto component firms produce several related items for final sales. Exports of those items can somewhat dampen/reverse the net 'substitutability' effect of manufacturing-OFDI.

3.2 *Technological variables*

Vehicle manufacturers involve their direct suppliers in designing the critical components. The effects of in-house R&D and technology import on 'OEM-Level exporter' and 'OEM/Tier-Level exporter' status are of special interest to us. Access to the technical collaborator's marketing intelligence and networks can facilitate achieving this status. R&D leads to newer products and lower production cost. For India, Pradhan (2007) and Singh (2009) indicate a favourable effect of R&D on exports, while Singh (2006) applying two-stage least-squares estimation finds complementarity between R&D and exports.

The R&D intensity in relation to sales, *RDint_C* is measured considering only the current (non-capital) R&D expenses, as it is generally more stable over time compared to the R&D capital expenses component. We consider tech-import as: *TCno*, number of foreign technical agreements; *TechMint*, technology import (remittances) intensity; and *EmbTechMint*, (capital goods) embodied technology import intensity; these variables are not significantly pair-wise correlated. We also estimate the effects of *Skill* of employees, and intangible and computer/IT assets intensities, *INTANint* and *Comp/ITint*.

3.3 *Marketing capabilities and efforts*

Marketing capabilities play an indirect role too, via the innovation success (Lefebvre and Lefebvre 2002). Besides industry journals advertisement, auto component firms participate in Auto Expo, Buyer-Supplier meets, etc. We examine the effects of advertisement intensity, *ADint*, and 1–0 dummy variables: the environmental management system *ISO14001* and *Emark* certifications, *Trademark* and *Xincharge* (exports-incharge).[4] Among 124 sample firms, 84 (67.74%) have ISO14001 certification; notably almost all (118) firms are quality management system ISO/TS16949-certified. The Emark and CEmark – product certifications for European Union (EU) standards for safety, health and environmental protection – apply to automotive and electronic products, respectively; vehicles contain many electronic items.[5] *Emark* is 'Emark and/or CEmark' certification dummy. International management standards and product certifications act as marketing tools, especially for international business.

3.4 *Productivity*

The 'exports vs. horizontal OFDI' literature examines the role of productivity. The least productive firms confine to domestic sales while others serve foreign markets too; more productive exporters undertake OFDI (Helpman, Melitz, and Yeaple 2004). Among OFDI firms, the productivity and geographic spread of OFDI are associated (Tanaka 2012). Also, both exports and OFDI lead to productivity dynamism paths (Merino 2012). Export competitiveness requires not just technical but multi-faceted efficiency of operations, and we employ profitability as a proxy variable. For our sample of exporters, we expect the gross profit margin on sales, *PM_G* to have a positive partial effect on total exports. The cost efficiency may have a minor influence on the exporter status (*XerO* and *XerOT*).

3.5 *Miscellaneous variables*

We estimate the effect of corporate foreign equity ownership, *FE*(%), representing the collaborator's stake in the affiliate-profitability. We employ minority and majority foreign ownership dummies (*MINFD, MAJFD*), or (*FD, FEadj*, and *FEadj2*) variables. FD is $\geq$10% FE dummy; FEadj = (FE − 10) for inward-FDI firms. Else, we distinguish between the effects of Japanese and non-Japanese collaborator nationality (*FC_Japan, FC_~Japan*); Japanese industrial buyers are known to be relatively more stringent. Table 4 later provides the sample information on firm-ownership by categories.

For a business group (BG) affiliated firm, the derived resources and network externalities from its group associates engaged in related downstream/upstream activities may facilitate its internationalization (Singh 2011).[6] We expect a favourable effect of Indian business group-affiliation (*BG*) on exports, as found by Singh (2009), and on the exporter status. Alternatively, we explore the influence of the stock of 'overseas investment in group companies' to total assets ratio, *OIGint*.

The effect of log-sales (*SizesL*) on log-experts tests the size-proportionality of exports. The special requirements of OEM and Tier-1 supplies, mentioned above, involve scale economies. Moreover, vehicle MNEs practise vendor rationalisation, and assess the prospective vendor's 'regional/global supplier' potential. Hence, larger firms are more likely to be OEM-Level exporters.

For firm-age we employ the variable log of age since production commencement, *AgeL*. The exports facilitating effect of accumulated learning and experience is likely to taper off. Since the 1990s, there have been far-reaching changes in the emission and safety norms for vehicles, and technological advances in manufacturing of modules and sub-modules. Therefore, relatively young auto component firms (establishments) may have a competitive edge to target international OEMs and high-Tier buyers.

4. The sample, data and the industry

4.1 *The sample and data sources*

This study employs firm-level data sourced from the Centre for Monitoring Indian Economy (CMIE), Prowess database for public listed companies (NIC code 30913) and a publication by the industry association Automotive Component Manufacturers Association of India (ACMA),[7] covering a few non-members too. We extracted the intersecting set of primarily automotive component producers. The Prowess data for company's standalone operations pertain to financial year April to March 2010–2011, or ending later in 2011. After excluding the non-exporters due to the small proportion (12 out of 136 firms), we have a sample of 124 producer–exporters. It is essentially a sample of large and medium-sized auto component firms, and there is ample intra-sample variability of firm-size and other explanatory variables.[8] The firm-level OFDI data, available from July 2007 onwards, are from the Reserve Bank of India (RBI) website. The Overseas Investment Division of RBI compiles the OFDI data reported by authorized dealers, as financial commitments in the form of equity, loans and guarantees issued (US$).[9] Table 1 presents the variables and definitions.

4.2 *The industry*

The global production of cars and commercial vehicles fell by 16% during 2007–2009, far more in USA and Japan (Source: www.oica.net). For India, the remarkable expansion of turnover and exports of auto components in the mid-2000s was somewhat contained by the recent global recession. This is evident by comparing the compound annual growth rate (CAGR) of a few years prior and subsequent to the recession (Table 2). However, the medium-term prospects seem bright. The Indian automobile industry witnessed high growth rates of production and exports during 2007–2008 to 2011–2012.

Table 1. Variables and definitions.

Variable	Definition
Exports-related variables	
ExportsL	Log_e of exports of goods in Rs. Lakhs
XerO	Exporter to OEMs 1–0 dummy
XerOT	Exporter to 'OEMs and/or Tier-firms' 1–0 dummy
OFDI-related variables	
OFDIEint	OFDI-equity investment intensity (%); 'yearly average OFDI-equity investment flow during July 2007 to March 2012' as ratio to current sales in dollars (during 2010–2011); *OFDIEint2* is OFDIEint-square
OFDIint	OFDI investment intensity (%); defined as OFDIEint, except OFDI as equity plus loans and guarantees issued; *OFDIint2* is OFDIint-square
OFDIE_Asset	OFDI-equity investment to total assets ratio (%); total OFDI-equity flow during July 2007 to March 2012 as ratio to year-end 2010–2011 total assets in dollars; *OFDIE_Asset2* is square of OFDIE_Asset
OFDInoC	Number of OFDI-countries
OFDInoE_Mfg	Number of enterprises in which OFDI undertaken as manufacturing activity
OFDInoE_~Mfg	Number of enterprises in which non-manufacturing OFDI undertaken
Foreign collaboration variables	
FC_Japan, FC_~Japan	Japanese and non-Japanese financial collaboration 1–0 dummies; if >1 collaborator, the higher (highest) ownership collaborator considered
FD	Financial collaboration 1–0 dummy (equity ownership by foreign corporate bodies, FE ≥10%)
FEadj	FE adjusted = FE – 10 if FD = 1, else zero; FEadj2 is FE adjusted-square
MAJFD, MINFD	Majority (>50%) and Minority (10–50%) foreign equity 1–0 dummies
Technology acquisition variables	
RDint_C	R&D current expenses intensity (%); ratio to sales
TCno	Number of technical collaborations; ongoing pure-technical and tech-cum-financial foreign collaborations
TechMint	Technology import intensity (%); ratio of foreign exchange remittances as royalty, technical fees and licensing fees to value of Output (= Sales, plus addition to stock of finished goods, minus purchase of finished goods and outsourced manufacturing jobs)
EmbTechMint	Embodied technology import intensity (%); ratio of import of capital goods to value of Output
Marketing variables	
Adint	Advertisement expenses intensity (%); ratio to Sales
Emark	Emark (or CEmark) certification 1–0 dummy
ISO14001	ISO14001 certification 1–0 dummy
Trademark	Trademark 1–0 dummy
Xincharge	Exports Incharge 1–0 dummy
Other miscellaneous variables	
AgeL	Log_e of age in 2011 as years since commencement of production (age truncated to 50 years; a few cases)
BG	Indian business group affiliation 1–0 dummy
Comp/ITint	'Computer/IT systems assets' intensity (%); ratio to gross fixed assets
Gsales	Growth rate of sales (%)
INTANint	Intangible assets intensity; ratio to gross fixed assets (%)
OIGint	'Overseas investment in Group companies' intensity (%); stock of these investments (in equity and preference shares and debt instruments) as ratio to total assets of the investing firm
PM_G	Gross profit margin (%); ratio of 'profits before interest, tax, depreciation and amortization' to total income; both net of prior period and extra-ordinary income
SizesL	Log_e of size as sales in Rs. crores
Skill	Skill level; compensation to employees (Rs. crores)/no of employees

Table 2.   Indian automotive industry output and exports in recent years.

	2007–2008	2008–2009	2009–2010	2010–2011	2011–2012	2015–2016(E)	2020–2021(E)	CAGR (%) 2007–2008 to 2011–2012	CAGR (%) 2004–2005 to 2007–2008
Auto Components	($ Billion)								
Turnover	26.5	23.0	30.1	39.9	43.5	66.3	113.0	13.19	27.42
Exports	3.8	4.0	3.4	5.2	6.8	12.3	29.0	15.66	27.71
Automobiles	(Number in thousands)								
Production	10,854	11,172	14,057	17,892	20,366			17.04	8.63
Exports	1238	1531	1804	2320	2910			23.82	25.25

Data Sources: For auto components: Status_Indian_Auto_Industry.pdf accessed from www.acma.in on 15 September 2011 and 29 April 2013.
For automobiles: www.siam.in, Industry Statistics accessed on 12 April 2011 and 1 May 2013.

The total equity-OFDI outflow from India by automotive firms during July 2007 to March 2012 has been $4633 million, of which $570 million and $4063 million outflow is by auto component and vehicle firms (Table 3). Thus, the yearly average equity-OFDI is 975, 120, and 855 dollar millions. The average OFDI among outward investors is, as expected, relatively far higher for vehicle firms. While the wholly owned subsidiary mode is predominant for auto component firms, the automobile firms have opted for this and joint venture modes of investment with similar frequency. Only about half the OFDI enterprises of auto component firms have manufacturing activity; the vehicle sector OFDI is almost entirely manufacturing-OFDI. These differences are expected due to: vehicle exports facing heavier transport cost and trade restrictions; much costlier plants for vehicles; and local variations in tastes and preferences for vehicles.

Long time-series data on Indian automotive sector OFDI are unavailable. Pradhan and Singh (2009) report $1129.2 million disclosed value of acquisitions during 2002 to March 2008. The estimated greenfield investment during 1970–1999 was mere $17.9 million. During 2000 to March 2007, excluding April 2001 to September 2002, the greenfield investment was $730.5

Table 3.   OFDI by Indian automotive firms (cumulative July 2007 to March 2012).

	Auto component firms (of these, sample firms)		Vehicle firms	All firms
Number of firms having equity-OFDI	47	(19)	8	55
Number of firms having OFDI (equity/loans/guarantees issued)	51	(21)	8	59
Total equity-OFDI (US$ million)	570.02	(139.25)	4062.84	4632.86
Total OFDI (US$ million)	979.73	(510.99)	6093.40	7073.13
Number of OFDI enterprises	80	(38)	29	109
Wholly owned Subsidiaries	67	(33)	15	82
Joint ventures	13	(5)	14	27
Number of manufacturing OFDI enterprises	39	(18)	26	65
Number of non-manufacturing OFDI enterprises	41	(20)	3	44

Source: Compiled from the RBI website www.rbi.org.in

million, and of this, $164.4 million was by auto component firms. Thus, the yearly average OFDI since 2007–2008 seems substantially higher.

5. OFDI vs. other firms: a comparison

Out of 124 firms in our sample, one-sixth (21) firms have undertaken OFDI during July 2007 to March 2012 (Tables 3 and 4). Among these, 19 firms have undertaken equity-OFDI and 2 firms had OFDI only as loans or guarantees issued. During this period they have invested in 38 foreign enterprises (sometimes repeatedly). A large majority of these foreign enterprises is wholly owned subsidiaries (33). About half of the OFDI enterprises (18) are engaged in manufacturing activity, the remaining being mostly in trading/distribution activities.

Table 4.   OFDI vs. other firms in the sample: a comparison.

	Equity-OFDI firms	Firms without equity-OFDI	Total-OFDI firms	Firms without OFDI	Total sample[a]
Number of firms, of which	19	105	21	103	124
(i) Indian-owned	11	71	12	70	82
(ii) Minority foreign [Japanese + Others]	6 [5 + 1]	20 [9 + 11]	7 [5 + 2]	19 [9 + 10]	26 [14 + 12]
(iii) Majority foreign [Japanese + Others]	2 [1 + 1]	14 [4 + 10]	2 [1 + 1]	14 [4 + 10]	16 [5 + 11]
Simple averages					
OFDI variables					
OFDI-equity Investment Intensity, *OFDIEint* (%)	0.830	0	0.751	0	0.127
OFDI investment Intensity, *OFDIint* (%)	1.574	0.073	1.791	0	0.303
OFDI-equity investment to total assets ratio, *OFDIE_Asset* (%)	4.233	0	3.830	0	0.649
Total OFDI investment/total assets (%)	7.952	0.079	7.592	0	1.286
Other variables					
Sales (Rs. crores)	1208.5	511.3***	1192.4	501.1***	618.14
R&D total expenses to sales ratio (%)	0.86	0.38**	0.78	0.38**	0.45
R&D current expenses Intensity, *RDint_C* (%)	0.58	0.28**	0.54	0.28*	0.32
Tech-import intensity, *TechMInt* (%)	0.26	0.30	0.24	0.31	0.30
Foreign Tech-collaborations No., *TCno*	1.74	0.84*	1.90	0.79**	0.98
Gross profit margin (%), *PM_G*	14.86	10.50**	15.64	10.26***	11.17
Exports of goods to sales ratio (%)	15.27	11.40	14.34	11.51	11.99
OEM-Level exporter firms, *XerO* ratio	0.737	0.600	0.762	0.592	0.621
OEM/Tier exporter firms, *XerOT* ratio	0.842	0.714	0.857	0.709*	0.734
Proportion of firms associated with Indian BGs	0.526	0.629	0.524	0.631	0.613

[a]The OFDI firms are those having undertaken OFDI any time in recent years (July 2007 to March 2012).
*Indicate 10% level of significance.
**Indicate 5% level of significance.
***Indicate 1% level of significance for *t*-test for difference of means.

Comparing the equity-OFDI and total-OFDI firms with the respective remaining sample firms (Table 4) reveals that those firms which have undertaken OFDI in recent years are, on an average, relatively much bigger, as expected, and have substantially higher R&D intensity while similar average technology import intensity (*t*-test applied). However, the average number of ongoing foreign technical collaborations (TCno) is significantly higher for them; 16 out of 21 total-OFDI firms (14 out of 19 equity-OFDI firms) have one or more ongoing foreign technical collaboration, as against 38 out of 103 non-OFDI firms.

The mean profitability (PM_G) of OFDI-undertaking enterprises is relatively high. The OFDI firms have higher average export intensity, and the 'Level' of exports, XerO and XerOT; but these differences are statistically weak. Surprisingly, the incidence of Indian BG affiliation is not higher among the OFDI firms.

For equity-OFDI firms, the average ratio of 'equity-OFDI flow during July 2007 to March 2012' to total assets of the investing firm is 4.23% while the mean value of total OFDI flow (including loans and guarantees issued) to total assets ratio is 7.95% (Table 4). Similarly their average OFDI intensity, measured as ratio of 'yearly average' outward-FDI to sales, is not negligible. Moreover, some part of the OFDI may be actually financed outside the home country.

6. Analysis of results

Estimates of the preferred specifications are presented in Tables 5–7. Judging by the variance-inflation-factor, the multicollinearity is not high for the sample.

6.1 *Being exporter to OEMs, XerO equation*

The OFDI-equity intensity, OFDIEint has an expected inverted U-shaped effect on the OEM-Level export participation, i.e. on being exporter from Home to OEMs (Table 5). The relationship is positive for the sample range of OFDIEint, barring the two largest values 5.223% and 3.667%. Similar tendencies emerge for the total OFDI intensity, OFDIint measure employed experimentally (Equation 2). The estimated relationship is inverted U-shaped also with the measure equity-OFDI to assets ratio, OFDIE_Asset (Equation 3). The three largest sample values of OFDIE_Asset exceed the value up to which the effect is positive. Among the equity-OFDI firms, $r(OFDIEint, OFDIE\_Asset) = +0.963$; accordingly, the results are similar for these two alternative measures (first and last Equations, Tables 5–7).

The number of manufacturing and non-manufacturing OFDI enterprises, i.e. OFDInoE_Mfg and OFDInoE_~Mfg variables have opposite effects which are both large and significant. The estimated coefficients indicate that the unfavourable effect of manufacturing OFDI enterprises far exceeds the favourable effect of non-manufacturing OFDI enterprises. Alternative specifications substituting these two variables with the total number of OFDI enterprises indicated consistently negative but generally insignificant effect. However, the variable OFDInoC – number of OFDI countries, indicating the OFDI geographical diversification – has a significant negative influence on the probability of OEM-exporter status, XerO (Equation 2).

Thus, our findings relating to the effect of OFDI on the probability of the investing firm being OEM-Level exporter indicate support for the complementarity hypothesis. An increase in outward-FDI (ratio to sales or assets) up to a moderate level of OFDI intensity and a larger number of non-manufacturing-OFDI enterprises enhance this likelihood. However, having a larger number of manufacturing-OFDI enterprises or of OFDI-countries reduce this likelihood; again, in the range of sizeable OFDI intensity, a higher OFDI intensity decreases this probability. These results point to the substitutability influence of a deeper global integration by the MNE.

Table 5. Logistic regression estimates of OEM-level export participation, XerO.

Explan. Var.↓	Equation 1	Equation 2	N = 124 Equation 3
SizesL	0.897 (2.75)***	0.850 (2.59)***	0.902 (2.76)***
AgeL	−1.287 (2.37)**	−1.261 (2.26)**	−1.270 (2.34)**
ISO14001	1.632 (2.27)**	1.667 (2.28)**	1.640 (2.27)**
Xincharge	2.109 (2.83)***	2.236 (2.90)***	2.146 (2.88)***
TechMint	−1.537 (2.80)***	−1.510 (2.54)**	−1.528 (2.78)***
Adint	2.635 (2.90)***	2.457 (2.60)***	2.621 (2.84)***
Gsales	−0.028 (2.10)**	−0.024 (1.88)*	−0.027 (2.03)**
OFDIEint	17.051 (3.84)***		
OFDIEint2	−4.3683 (3.46)***		
OFDIint		18.303 (2.88)***	
OFDIint2		−2.376 (2.93)***	
OFDIE_Asset			4.930 (3.54)***
OFDIE_Asset2			−0.3754 (3.23)***
OFDInoC		−3.459 (3.05)***	
OFDInoE_Mfg	−5.508 (4.02)***		−5.352 (4.07)***
OFDInoE_~Mfg	2.193 (3.61)***		1.617 (3.35)***
TCno	0.433 (2.10)**	0.439 (1.97)**	0.432 (2.08)**
FEadj	0.083 (2.27)**	0.075 (1.96)**	0.082 (2.24)**
FEadj2	−0.0016 (2.74)***	−.0015 (2.46)**	−0.0016 (2.71)***
RDint_C	−1.647 (1.78)*	−1.507 (1.88)*	−1.661 (1.79)*
EmbTechMint	−0.204 (1.63)	−0.213 (1.73)*	−0.204 (1.63)
Emark	1.677 (1.40)	2.036 (1.65)*	1.698 (1.40)
Comp/ITint	−0.309 (1.55)	−0.302 (1.54)	−0.310 (1.55)
Constant	−1.601 (0.82)	−1.662 (0.84)	−1.728 (0.90)
Psuedo R^2	0.4069	0.3907	0.4054
Wald χ^2 (df)	49.12 (18)	32.70 (17)	44.89 (18)
Prob> χ^2	0.0001	0.0123	0.0004

Note: Robust Z-values for b-coefficients.
*Indicate 10% level of significance.
**Indicate 5% level of significance.
***Indicate 1% level of significance.

The effect of technological variables is mixed. A significant positive effect of number of technical collaborations, TCno indicates the higher probability of bagging OEM contract(s) with an ongoing foreign technical collaboration, more so with multiple ones (with the same or different collaborators). But the technology import (remittances) intensity, TechMint has a significant negative effect. Perhaps in case of relatively sophisticated technology the foreign technical collaborators may be discouraging (restricting subtly) during the collaboration period any exports to OEMs or high-Tier buyers. Intriguingly, even in-house R&D intensity, *RDint_C* appears to reduce the probability of being OEM-Level exporter, an unexpected tendency, *albeit* weak. Singh (2010) found a positive but statistically insignificant effect of having an R&D-Incharge on the probability of exports to OEMs or to 'OEMs/high Tier-Level' firms during 2004–2005. We find that even the capital goods import intensity and computer/IT assets intensity (EmbTech-Mint and Comp/ITint) have negative effects, though weak. The effect of Skill variable was insignificant.

A few observations are pertinent to the year in question, i.e. 2010–2011. The recent global recession affected adversely the vehicle demand in industrialized countries. It curtailed their imports of auto components for vehicle manufacturing, and perhaps the development of new vehicles and their critical components. In the recent past auto component producers in India

Table 6.   Logistic regression estimates of OEM/Tier-Level export participation, XerOT.

Explan. Var.↓	Equation 1	Equation 2	Equation 3	$N=124$ Equation 4
SizesL	0.473 (1.30)	0.586 (1.55)	0.482 (1.30)	0.475 (1.30)
ISO14001	2.106 (2.90)***	2.168 (2.81)***	2.165 (2.95)***	2.110 (2.91)***
Xincharge	1.589 (2.04)**	1.829 (2.51)**	1.607 (2.04)**	1.586 (2.04)**
TechMint	−1.799 (2.41)**	−1.891 (2.63)***	−1.838 (2.44)**	−1.804 (2.42)**
Adint	1.998 (2.05)**	2.336 (2.47)**	2.014 (2.05)**	1.997 (2.04)**
OFDIEint	12.602 (3.33)***	12.319 (2.96)***	57.377 (2.51)**	
OFDIEint2	−3.0769 (4.47)***	−3.0400 (4.18)***	−11.1623 (2.59)***	
OFDIE_Asset				2.672 (2.22)**
OFDIE_Asset2				−0.1299 (3.06)***
OFDInoC			−2.572 (2.01)**	
OFDInoE_Mfg	−2.406 (1.97)**	−2.265 (1.62)		−2.437 (1.94)*
OFDInoE_~Mfg	14.200 (3.42)***	14.911 (3.67) ***		15.334 (3.57)***
FC_~Japan	2.052 (1.51)	2.019 (1.52)	2.071 (1.51)	2.057 (1.51)
RDint_C		−0.955 (0.87)		
Skill	−68.443 (2.20)**	−66.121 (2.09)**	−69.157 (2.19)**	−68.584 (2.20)**
Emark	1.761 (1.64)	2.176 (1.49)	1.875 (1.75)*	1.761 (1.64)
Comp/ITint	−0.474 (2.19)**	−0.557 (2.51)**	−0.478 (2.17)**	−0.474 (2.18)**
INTANint	0.119 (1.85)*	0.139 (1.89)*	0.119 (1.84)*	0.118 (1.84)*
Constant	−2.206 (1.21)	−2.848 (1.51)	−2.277 (−1.24)	−2.216 (1.22)
Psuedo R^2	0.4049	0.4161	0.3995	0.4044
Wald χ^2 (df)	87.76 (14)	93.06 (15)	77.72 (13)	92.93 (14)
Prob> χ^2	0.0000	0.0000	0.0000	0.0000

Note: Robust Z-values for b-coefficients.
*Indicate 10% level of significance.
**Indicate 5% level of significance.
***Indicate 1% level of significance.

might have focused their R&D and related activities mainly on the comparatively buoyant vehicle market at home; the variety and sophistication of vehicles sold domestically has enhanced dramatically. Nonetheless, there is a need to scrutinize the technology level of OEM and high Tier-Level exports of auto components from India.

The marketing efforts/capabilities seem to be quite important for the OEM-Level export participation. This is evident from the estimated coefficients for the variables advertisement intensity, exports-Incharge and ISO14001 certification. The Emark certification has a weak effect.

The foreign ownership dummy being highly insignificant was dropped. FEadj has an inverted U-shaped effect. The maximum value appears around 25–28% FEadj (i.e. 35–38% foreign equity). Thus, compared to locally owned firms, *ceteris paribus*, firms having high majority foreign equity (say ≥75%) are less likely to be OEM-Level exporter. Alternative formulations indicate the minority and majority, or Japanese and non-Japanese foreign ownership dummies being insignificant.

As expected, the firm size has a consistently significant favourable effect. *Ceteris paribus*, younger firms are more likely to be OEM-Level exporter. The growth rate of sales, Gsales has a negative impact; perhaps due to the global recession those exporting to OEMs might have faced low/negative growth rate of exports, lowering their total sales growth.

6.2   *Being exporter to OEMs and/or Tier-firms, XerOT equation*

As for the OEM-Level exporter status, similarly for being exporter to 'OEMs/Tier firms' the OFDI-equity intensity has an inverted U-shaped influence within the sample range of this

Table 7. Regression estimates of log-exports, ExportsL.

Explan. Var.↓	Equation 1	Equation 2	N = 124 Equation 3
SizesL	0.762 (5.01)***	0.783 (4.85)***	0.756 (4.98)***
AgeL	0.736 (2.88)***	0.658 (2.38)**	0.734 (2.86)***
BG		0.290 (0.97)	
OIGint	0.046 (2.04)**		0.044 (1.87)*
OFDIEint	0.409 (3.42)***	0.403 (2.22)**	
OFDIE_Asset			0.079 (3.12)***
OFDInoE_Mfg		0.121 (0.32)	
OFDInoE_~Mfg		0.087 (0.35)	
FC_Japan	−1.142 (2.84)***	−1.198 (2.98)***	−1.107 (2.78)***
RDInt_C	0.510 (1.80)*	0.516 (1.77)*	0.501 (1.77)*
Adint	0.429 (2.10)**	0.452 (2.20)**	0.424 (2.08)**
Trademark	0.714 (1.92)*	0.711 (1.83)*	0.717 (1.92)*
PM_G	0.044 (2.78)***	0.044 (2.59)***	0.046 (2.89)***
Constant	−0.891 (0.79)	−0.883 (0.71)	−0.869 (0.77)
R^2	0.4332	0.4281	0.4314
Adjusted-R^2	0.3885	0.3719	0.3865
F-value	13.02	10.12	12.80
Prob>F	0.0000	0.0000	0.0000

Note: Robust t-values for b-coefficients.
*Indicate 10% level of significance.
**Indicate 5% level of significance.
***Indicate 1% level of significance.

intensity (Table 6). The alternative measure equity-OFDI to total assets ratio, OFDIE_Asset indicates the same tendency (Equation 4). The number of OFDI countries has a negative influence. The number of manufacturing and of non-manufacturing OFDI enterprises have, respectively, negative and positive effects. However, as a remarkable difference, the favourable effect of non-manufacturing OFDI enterprises is stronger and more significant than the unfavourable effect of manufacturing OFDI enterprises on 'OEM/Tier-Level' export participation.

While the number of foreign technical collaborations and capital goods import intensity coefficients are insignificant (results not tabulated), a significant negative effect is found for the technology import (remittances) intensity, and also for the computer/IT assets intensity and Skill variables. The R&D intensity coefficient is negative but quite weak. Incidentally the intangible assets (copyrights etc.) intensity, INTANint has a favourable effect.

For both the OEM-exporter status and for OEM/Tier-exporter status (XerO and XerOT variables), the role of marketing factors is similarly important. However, the effect of firm size, though positive, is weak; and the growth of sales and age variables are not significant determinants of OEM/Tier-Level export participation. The foreign ownership is seen to be inconsequential; the only notable tendency is a weak favourable effect of non-Japanese foreign ownership (FC_~Japan).

6.3 Exports-log, ExportsL equation

All the estimated equations are statistically significant, as judged by the F-value (Table 7). The OFDIEint variable has a positive, large and highly significant effect; the OFDIEint-square variable was insignificant and dropped. Thus, an increase in the OFDI-equity investment intensity consistently enhances the total exports. A similar favourable effect emerges with the alternative measure 'equity-OFDI to total assets ratio', OFDIE_Asset. The complementary effect of OFDI on the parent company's total exports from the home country is in conformity with the existing evidence, in general. Even the intensity of overseas investment in group companies (OIGint) has a perceptible favourable effect. The BG association *per se* tends to increase the firm's total exports but the tendency is statistically weak.[10] Given the equity-OFDI intensity, neither the number of OFDI countries nor that of total OFDI enterprises exerts a significant effect (these results not tabulated). Even separately the number of manufacturing and of non-manufacturing OFDI enterprises fail to acquire any conventional level of significance.

The R&D intensity, RDint_C coefficient is consistently positive in log-exports equations; it is large and significant – at 5% level if one applies the 'appropriate' one (right)-tail test. Thus, more R&D intensive firms seem to enjoy greater export competitiveness, corroborating the previous evidence for India. The other technological variables have been dropped due to insignificance.

Among the marketing variables, the advertisement intensity and trademark have significant favourable effects and these are sizable. The firm profitability has a large positive partial effect on its total exports, though it does not influence the exporter status. Thus, more productive firms have higher value of total exports – a noteworthy finding for an 'exclusively exporters' sample.

The foreign ownership variables are insignificant, except the FC_Japan dummy. Compared to other firms, the Japanese-owned firms seem to export less, apparently being more focused on the Indian domestic market. Bigger firms export more. The estimated SizesL coefficient, indicating the elasticity of exports with respect to total sales, is below unity, as found by Singh (2010). Firms having greater production-experience, i.e. older firms export more.[11]

By way of magnitudes, the outward-FDI and in-house R&D intensities appear to have considerable favourable influence on the export performance of the firm. The explained variable being log-exports, we find antilog of b-coefficients (Table 7, Equations 1 and 3). An increase in equity-OFDI intensity (%) by 1.0 raises the estimated exports by about 50%; for a small change (Δ) in *OFDIEint*, namely $\Delta OFDIEint = 0.2$, the estimated effect on exports is 8.5% (Equation 1). Alternatively (Equation 3), a unit increase in 'equity-OFDI to total assets (%)', i.e. $\Delta OFDIE\_Asset = 1.0$ increases the exports by 8.2%. An inter-firm difference of one percentage-point in R&D current expenses intensity ($\Delta RDInt\_C = 1$) increases the exports by about two-thirds; $\Delta RDInt\_C = 0.5$ increases the exports by approximately 29%.

7. Conclusions

This section summarizes the main findings and offers a few policy suggestions. This empirical study guards against viewing the OFDI as a homogenous entity. The manufacturing and non-manufacturing OFDI may have dissimilar implications for the MNE's home operations, like the probabilities of being OEM-Level and OEM/Tier-Level exporter.

We find support for the OFDI-exports complementarity hypothesis, given the consistent favourable effect of the OFDI intensity on total exports from Home (facilities) by the parent company. It also implies that the OFDI enlarges the MNE's global scale of operations. Again there are positive effects of OFDI intensity up to a certain limit and of the number of non-manufacturing OFDI enterprises on the OEM-Level and OEM/Tier-Level export participations.

Pradhan (2007) recommends a proactive strategy towards OFDI as an engine of exports growth. Based on our findings, we prescribe the same also for moving up the international value chains. This is not to deny the importance of other measures like cost-competitiveness of domestic operations for export promotion purposes.

Our results also point to some noteworthy elements of the OFDI-exports substitutability in case of a high degree of OFDI-internationalization. An increase in OFDI intensity beyond a certain level, and greater number of manufacturing-OFDI enterprises and of total OFDI-countries reduce the likelihood of OEM-Level and OEM/Tier-Level export participations. Here, we may add that the manufacturing-OFDI enterprises may supply to some international OEMs or high-Tier customers – such disaggregate sales figures are not available – in lieu of the parent company exporting to those firms from Home. However, that should not be construed as a decline in global competitiveness of the MNE's home country operations. The parent company is still likely to be involved in the mutual learning through component designing and modifications for these international buyers.

As regards the impact of technological variables, the number of foreign technical collaborations has a favourable impact on the probability of being exporter to OEMs. A higher R&D intensity leads to higher total exports but not greater probability of exporting to OEMs or to 'OEMs and/or Tier-firms'; in fact, it has a weak adverse effect on the OEM-Level export participation. Higher technology import intensity reduces these two probabilities and does not even increase the total exports – indicative of the prevalence of subtle export restrictions.

By way of enhancing the R&D and technology intensity of auto component exports from India to OEMs, we suggest the following. The government must strengthen value chains in India, and ensure that the just-in-time (or quick) export delivery of tech-intensive modules and sub-modules, as stipulated by global OEMs and high-Tier buyer-firms, does not face infrastructural export bottlenecks. Considering the role of R&D, encouraging SMEs to have in-house R&D and testing facilities would increase their exports.

This study finds the firm-level marketing capabilities and efforts to be important determinants of its export competitiveness, even in terms of the OEM or high-Tier supply linkages. The ISO14001 certification facilitates these linkages. This finding is pertinent to designing national policies for promoting the adoption of international standards. In our sample of exporters, the more profitable firms export more. This highlights indirectly the role of productivity in explaining inter-firm variations in export performance even within an exclusively exporters group.

As limitations of the study we must mention that while OFDI can have many ramifications for the home as well as host nations and firms, our cross-section investigation is confined only to the exports from Home by the investing firm. Taking into account the endogeneity of OFDI, and estimating the dynamic effects of OFDI intensity and OFDI-type would have been more informative and challenging too. Even R&D intensity and productivity have theoretically two-way relationships with exports (Damijan, Kostevc, and Polanec 2010). The data limitations prevented us from analysing the value of exports to OEMs or to OEMs/Tier-firms. Our exports analysis based on data for 2010–2011 might have been affected by the aftermath of the global recession. The suggestions for future research are: incorporating the potential improvements, as implied above, and extending the analysis to other countries and sectors.

Acknowledgement

I am extremely grateful to the two referees for their incisive comments and valuable suggestions. The usual disclaimer applies.

Notes

1. During 2006–2011, the world share of developing nations in total FDI outflows was 19.56%, with India's share being 0.98%. In case of cross-border mergers and acquisitions (M&As) value, developing countries accounted for 18.46% share, with India's share being 2.37%. The respective shares in capital

investment in greenfield OFDI projects were 27.27% and 2.72%. Cross-border M&As formed about one-third of OFDI flow from developing nations (compiled from UNCTAD 2012).

2.   Many OFDI and/or exports studies refer to the (customer) 'proximity-concentration' (fixed costs of plant location and other scale economies) trade-off.

3.   The OEM-supplies can be used partly for aftermarket sales by OEMs (Singh 2010, fn. 3).

4.   Award 1–0 dummy – having Deming/JIPM/TPM Excellence Award or Ford Q1 certification – was insignificant in preliminary regressions.

5.   Globally the share of electronics in vehicle cost, 15% in 2004, may be as large as 40% in 2015 (ACMA 2012, 19).

6.   We have a high proportion of Indian BG-associated firms, particularly among minority-foreign firms. It is 62%, 81%, and 25% among local, minority, and majority foreign-owned firms, respectively; the sample average is 61%.

7.   ACMA, 'Buyers Guide 2012', Automotive Component Manufacturers Association of India, Delhi, 2012; the electronic CD is entitled 'Source India'.

8.   The sales range is 6–7722 rupee crores during 2010–2011; the 5–95% range is 53–1824 rupee crores; the mean is Rs. 347 crores (note: 100 lakhs = 10 millions = 1 crore). A high degree of positive skewness of firm-size distribution is also true of the overall auto component industry.

9.   The financial year 2010–2011 average and year-end rupee-US$ exchange rate was, respectively, 45.5768 and 44.6450.

10.   The variables OIGint and BG have insignificant coefficients in preliminary XerO and XerOT equations.

11.   The effect of vertical integration was insignificant.

References

ACMA (Automotive Component Manufacturers Association of India). 2012. *Auto Component Industry – Ready for the 'Transition': Leveraging Superior Growth Foresight to Strengthen Country Competitiveness.* Discussion Document, New Delhi: ACMA. http://acmainfo.com/docmgr/ACMA_AGM_2012_Presentations/Mckinsey_ACMA_presentation_5th_September_2012.pdf

Blonigen, B. A. 2001. "In Search of Substitution Between Foreign Production and Exports." *Journal of International Economics* 53 (1): 81–104.

Damijan, J. P., C. Kostevc, and S. Polanec. 2010. "From Innovation to Exporting or Vice Versa?" *The World Economy* 33 (3): 374–398.

Egger, P. 2001. "European Exports and Outward Foreign Direct Investment: A Dynamic Panel Data Approach." *Weltwirtschaftliches Archiv* 137 (3): 427–449.

Fonseca, M., A. Mendonça, and J. Passos. 2010. *Home Country Trade Effects of Outward FDI: An Analysis of the Portuguese Case, 1996–2007.* FEP Working Papers No. 365, Porto: University of Porto – Faculty of Economics.

Gereffi, G., and J. Lee. 2012. "Why the World Suddenly Cares about Global Supply Chains." *Journal of Supply Chain Management* 48 (3): 24–32.

Head, K., and J. Ries. 2001. "Overseas Investment and Firm Exports." *Review of International Economics* 9 (1): 108–122.

Helpman, E., M. J. Melitz, and S. R. Yeaple. 2004. "Export Versus FDI with Heterogeneous Firms." *The American Economic Review* 94 (1): 300–316.

Lefebvre, E., and L. A. Lefebvre. 2002. "Innovative Capabilities as Determinants of Export Performance and Behaviour: A Longitudinal Study of Manufacturing SMEs." In *Innovation and Firm Performance: Econometric Explorations of Survey Data*, edited by A. Kleinknecht and P. Mohnen, 281–309. New York: Palgrave.

Lipsey, R. E., and M. Y. Weiss. 1984. "Foreign Production and Exports of Individual Firms." *Review of Economics and Statistics* 66 (2): 304–307.

Merino, F. 2012. "Firms' Internationalization and Productivity Growth." *Research in Economics* 66 (4): 349–354.

Narayanan, K., and S. Bhat. 2010. "Technological Efforts and Export Performance of IT Firms in India." In *Indian and Chinese Enterprises: Global Trade, Technology and Investment Regimes*, edited by N. S. Siddharthan and K. Narayanan, 241–269. London: Routledge.

Neary, J. P. 2009. "Trade Costs and Foreign Direct Investment." *International Review of Economics & Finance* 18 (2): 207–218.

Pradhan, J. P. 2007. How do Indian Multinationals Affect Exports from Home Country? Working Paper No. 2007/07, April. Delhi: Institute for Studies in Industrial Development. (Also available as MPRA_paper_19022.pdf, December 2009).

Pradhan, J. P., and N. Singh. 2009. "Outward FDI and Knowledge Flows: A Study of the Indian Automotive Sector." *International Journal of Institutions and Economies* 1 (1): 155–186.

Singh, D. A. 2009. "Export Performance of Emerging Market Firms." *International Business Review* 18 (4): 321–330.

Singh, N. 2006. "R&D, Import of Technology and Trade Intensities: A Simultaneous Equation Micro-Level Examination." In *India: Industrialisation in a Reforming Economy – Essays for K L Krishna*, edited by S. Tendulkar, A. Mitra, K. Narayanan and D. Das, 471–491. New Delhi: Academic Foundation.

Singh, N. 2010. "Original Equipment Supply Chains and Auto Component Exports from India." In *Indian and Chinese Enterprises: Global Trade, Technology and Investment Regimes*, edited by N. S. Siddharthan and K. Narayanan, 270–301. London: Routledge.

Singh, N. 2011. "Emerging Economy Multinationals: The Role of Business Groups." *Economics, Management, and Financial Markets* 6 (1): 142–181.

Svensson, R. 1996. "Effects of Overseas Production on Home Country Exports: Evidence Based on Swedish Multinationals." *Weltwirtschaftliches Archiv* 132 (2): 304–329.

Swedenborg, B. 2001. "Determinants and Effects of Multinational Growth: The Swedish Case Revisited." In *Topics in Empirical International Economics: A Festschrift in Honor of Robert E. Lipsey*, edited by M. Blomstrom and L. S. Goldberg, 99–135. Chicago: University of Chicago Press.

Tanaka, A. 2012. "Firm Productivity and the Number of FDI Destinations: Evidence from a Non-Parametric Test." *Economics Letters* 117 (1): 1–3.

UNCTAD. 2012. *World Investment Report 2012: Towards a New Generation of Investment Policies*. New York: United Nations.

Technological determinants of firm-level technical efficiency in the Indian machinery industry[†]

Pradeep Kumar Keshari

Regional Training Centre, North, IDBI Bank Limited, Videocon Tower, Jhandewalan Extension, New Delhi, India

In the framework of resources-based view, a firm's performance is often defined in terms of its efficiency level in relation to other firms in an industry. Adopting this framework, the study examines the technological determinants of firm-level technical efficiency (TE) in the context of Indian machinery industry (IMI). It first computes the firm- and year-specific TE by estimating a stochastic frontier production function with the help of an unbalanced panel of data on a sample of 178 firms (with 940 observation) for seven years covering financial years from 2000/2001 to 2006/2007. Thereafter, the study analyses the determinants of firm-level TE by estimating a random-effect panel data model with Tobit specification. The study finds that a firm in the IMI could improve its TE by enhancing its technological *resources and capabilities* through attraction of foreign direct investment (FDI), import of disembodied technology, in-house research and development (R&D), import of intermediate goods and use of capital intensive techniques of production. In addition, it is also found that the larger size and younger firms; firms with higher networth intensity and higher product differentiation; firms based in less concentrated sub-industries of IMI are more efficient.[†]

1. Introduction

Indian machinery industry (IMI) represents *manufacture of machinery and equipment n.e.c.* that is the division 28 in *National Industrial Classification: All Economic Activities-*2008 (NIC-2008). It comprises two types of machinery producing industries, namely general purpose machinery (or group 281) and special purpose machinery (or group 282) at three digit level of NIC-2008. Following import substitution strategy of development, Government of India (GoI) promoted this industry (notably special purpose machinery segment of this industry) through public investment, as an important part of capital goods sector. As a result, production capacities were built in important segments of this industry. There are some evidence based on industry/enterprise surveys and data pertaining to the post-1991 reform period that the major part of capital goods industry: (a) has been unable to enhance its production capacity (in line with rising domestic demand for the same) and (b) lacks competitiveness even in comparison to the latecomers like China, Taiwan and South Korea due to: (i) the firm-specific factors like deficient technological capabilities, management and operational inefficiencies, inferior quality and finish of goods, lack of global market

---

[†]This is a revised version of a research article presented in seventh annual international conference 'Technology Intensity and Global Competitiveness' of Forum for Global Knowledge Sharing at Symbiosis, Pune.

orientation as well as (ii) external factors such as infrastructure bottlenecks, higher rate of interest, high incidence of indirect taxes, etc.; (c) has failed to address the challenges arising from the increasing imports of finished goods (viz. second-hand machinery) by the user industries (CII 2007; EXIM Bank 2008).

In post-World Trade Organization (WTO) era, restricting imports is neither possible nor desirable. Therefore, the IMI is required to develop additional production facilities with due focus on achieving international competitiveness so as to check the influx of imports. There is no denying that the external factors eclipsing international competitiveness of IMI need to be taken care of. Resource-based view (RBV) considers maximization of firm-level efficiency by judicious use of its internal resources (viz. intangible resources) to be the necessary condition for an industry to achieve international competitiveness (Peteraf and Barney 2003). Efficiency as an important indicator of firm-level performance has various connotations ranging from profitability, productivity, capacity utilization, allocative efficiency, TE, etc. This article employs firm-level TE as the indicator of efficiency and examines its determinants mainly following the theoretical framework of RBV. Among the probable determinants of TE, it focuses on the firm-specific technological factors. Empirical analysis of the study is conducted with the help of an unbalanced panel data of 940 observations on a sample of 178 firms belonging to IMI covering seven financial years (FYs) from 2000/2001 to 2006/2007. To compute firm- and year-specific technical efficiencies, the study estimates a stochastic frontier production function (SFPF).[1] In the SFPF framework, TE is defined as the ratio of a firm's actual output (conditional on a given combination of input levels and firm effects) to the corresponding (mean) output on the SFPF (i.e. when the firm could produce maximum output from the same combination of input levels) (Battese and Coelli 1992). To analyse the determinants of TE, we estimate a random-effect panel data model with Tobit specification.

Rest of the study is organized in six sections. Section 2 explains the status of IMI. Section 3 briefly discusses the theoretical framework, empirical literature and formulates verifiable hypothesis regarding the relationship between TE and its various determinants. Section 4 discusses the sample, period and data sources. Section 5 explains the econometric models and procedures for deriving TE and analysing the determinants of TE. Section 6 presents and discusses the findings of the empirical analysis. Section 7 offers conclusions.

2. IMI – the focus of study

Machinery industry, being capital, technology and skill intensive, has potential for being important source of innovations and higher value addition with higher margins and growth prospects as compared to the mature low-technology industries in which intense competition has shrunk margins and lowered growth prospects. The industry could also generate significant intra-industry and inter-industry externalities due to its linkages with other sectors of the economy. As the machinery industry supports the other sectors of economy and holds strategic importance, the Indian policy-makers, including those who laid the foundation for import-substitution industrialization in the early 1950s, considered the indigenous growth of this industry to be of paramount importance. Over the years, IMI grew manifold and started producing a wide range of machineries needed in various sectors of the economy.

The IMI constitutes about 3.76% weight in India's index of industrial production (base 2004/2005). In the market size of IMI (approximately Rs 90,000 crore) in the year 2006/2007, the share of exports constituted only about 11%, while the share of imports was 37%.[2] During the post-1991 reform period of August 1991 to July 2007, IMI has been relying heavily on import of disembodied technologies, but much less on foreign direct investment (FDI), for building its competitive advantage. As a result, IMI occupied the highest share of 16.6% in the cumulative number of foreign technological collaboration agreements (7886), followed by electrical equipment (15.9%) and chemicals (11.2%).[3] On the other hand, the IMI's share in cumulative inflow of FDI (Rs 28,364 crore) of manufacturing sector constituted only 5.1%, which compares poorly with the shares of other medium-/high-tech industries (viz. electrical equipments with 32% and transport equipments with 14%).[4]

Traditionally, the USA, Germany and Japan have been the largest suppliers of machinery. Of late, Asian countries such as China, South Korea and Taiwan have also emerged as the important players in the production and export of machineries. Consumption of IMI has also increased substantially in the developing Asian countries due to their thrust on the value-added manufacturing and sustained higher growth in their gross domestic product (GDP). The shifting base of machinery and equipment production from the developed to developing countries is also providing major opportunities of production and exports from technologically advanced countries of the developing economies like China, India, South Korea, etc. In the year 2005, countries like China and South Korea, respectively, shared 7% and 4% in the world's total production of IMI, while India's share was insignificant 1.4%, indicating ample scope for expansion in its market share (EXIM Bank 2008). Despite IMI's lack of global competitiveness as reflected in its low level of market share in the world production and exports, we do not find any econometric study exclusively focusing on the technological or other determinants of firm-specific efficiency in IMI. Identifying the determinants of firm-level efficiency is important as an industry achieves international competitiveness only by technical progress and sustained increases in efficiency and export shares of its constituent firms.

3. Analytical framework, empirical literature, explanatory variables and hypotheses

3.1 *Analytical framework*

This study mainly utilizes the RBV as the general framework for examining the technological determinants of firm-level TE. RBV provides an efficiency-based explanation to the firm-level performance, suggesting that a firm improves its performance by producing more and economically from the set of resources it holds and/or delivering greater benefits to the customer (e.g. better quality or differentiated goods) (Peteraf and Barney 2003).

The RBV looks for possible causes of inter-firm differences in performance mostly within their heterogeneous *resources and capabilities*, holding constant the characteristics of industry in which the firms operate. RBV is based on two major assumptions (Peteraf and Barney 2003): first, firms are heterogeneous or unique in terms of their *resources and capabilities* within industry. Second, resource heterogeneity may persist over time if the resources used for acquiring competitive advantages are rare, valuable, imperfectly imitable, imperfectly substitutable and imperfectly mobile in strategic factor markets.

The RBV divides resources into two major categories, namely *tangible assets* and *intangible assets*. The tangible assets may include financial assets (e.g. investments in securities, bank deposits and debtors) and physical assets (viz. land and building, plant, machinery and equipments and stocks). Intangible assets may consist of intellectual property (viz. patents, trade secrets, trademarks and brands), agreements and contracts, corporate image, networks and databases (Fahy and Smithee 1999). In comparison to tangible resources, *intangible assets* can be transferred easily from one unit to another and do not diminish by extra use; they are relatively resistant to duplication and difficult to be measured, valued and traded (Fahy and Smithee 1999). Hence, the intangible resources are more important source of heterogeneity and divergence in the performance of firms within an industry.

The capability is defined as a firm's capacity to effectively combine, integrate and coordinate a team of resources for achieving competitive advantage and better performance. A firm's unique capability may include automated systems for offering highly reliable services, development of a new product or process, manufacturing flexibility, responsiveness to market trends, short product development cycles, organizational culture of teamwork, good industrial relations, organizational routines and skills of individual or group (Fahy and Smithee 1999). It is difficult to delineate capabilities from intangible assets. Besides, it is difficult to segregate and measure them in an empirical study. Therefore, RBV researchers mostly include them into intangible assets.

3.2 *Empirical literature*

With regard to the manufacturing sector in the developing countries, there are not many studies on the determinants of TE but the numbers are growing. Some studies have focused on entire manufacturing sector, while others have focused on certain industries within the manufacturing sector. The studies have also focused on certain categories of explanatory variables and have used 'other' variables as the control variables. There are a few studies with exclusive focus on sources of technology (viz. Ray [2006] for India) and firm-specific knowledge (Wu et al. [2007] for China). Nevertheless, some studies have also used a few variables related to the technological factors while focusing on the effect of certain factors on the firm-specific TE. These empirical studies have reported capital intensity (Driffield and Kambhampati [2003] for India, Oczkowski and Sharma [2005] for Nepal, Wu et al. [2007] for China, Faruq and Yi [2010] for Ghana, Keshari [2012] for India), age (Ray [2006]; Bhandari and Maiti [2007] for India), exports intensity (Driffield and Kambhampati 2003; Goldar, Renganathan, and Banga 2004; Ray 2006), export propensity (Pham, Dao, and Reilly 2010), import of intermediate goods (Driffield and Kambhampati 2003; Goldar, Renganathan, and Banga 2004; Ray 2006; Keshari 2012), import of disembodied technology (Ray 2006), foreign ownership (Goldar, Renganathan, and Banga 2004; Faruq and Yi 2010; Keshari 2012) and research and development (R&D) intensity (Driffield and Kambhampati 2003; Wu et al. 2007; Keshari 2012) to be the important factors in explaining firm-level TE.

In terms of empirical methodology, Ray (2006) for India, Wu et al. (2007) for China and Faruq and Yi (2010) for Ghana have used data envelopment analysis (DEA) for computation of firm-specific TE. Driffield and Kambhampati (2003), Goldar, Renganathan, and Banga (2004), Bhandari and Maiti (2007) and Keshari (2012) for India; Oczkowski and Sharma (2005) for Nepal and Pham, Dao, and Reilly (2010) for Vietnam have estimated SFPF for computing the TE. For examining the determinants of TE, only two studies (viz. Wu et al. 2007 and Faruq and Yi 2010) have used more appropriate Tobit regression model which takes care of limiting characteristics (0< TE <1) of TE. Other scholars have analysed the determinants of TE by estimating variants of linear regression models either using cross section data or panel data.

3.3 *Explanatory variables and hypotheses*

RBV gives paramount importance to efficiency enhancing technological resources and capability. A firm in the machinery sector builds technology-based advantages majorly in the following manner: (i) through product innovations including design and drawings (basic as well as detailed) capabilities, (ii) through process innovation and production engineering including mastery of a range of manufacturing processes such as machining, welding, assembly and shop floor-based problem-solving related to the running, maintenance and repair of plants and (iii) by improving performance of machines and their components in terms of reliability, precision, durability and finish (CII 2007). These advantages and other related capabilities important for attaining superior efficiency can be built in a firm through: (a) FDI affiliations; (b) import of disembodied technology in an arm's length transaction; (c) import of intermediate goods (raw material, spare parts and capital goods) involving embodied technology; (d) deployment of capital intensive technologies; (e) exposure to international market through exports of final/semi-final goods and imports of intermediate goods; and (f) in-house research and development. It is therefore hypothesized that the technological resources and capabilities obtained through each of these avenues shall improve the firm-level TE. We now present detailed discussions on the relationship between TE and each explanatory variable used in the model.

3.3.1 *Technological variables*

FDI affiliation. FDI may play a major role in enhancing the efficiency of a firm in an industry in the host country for the following reasons (Dunning 2000): first, FDI affiliated firms (FAFs) may have access to efficiency enhancing *technology* and skills from their corresponding Multinational Enterprises networks and second, FAFs may also identify, evaluate and harness technology and skills present in the host country and combine these with their internal technological *capabilities* for maximizing the benefits of innovation, learning and accumulated knowledge. First and second together may lead to higher level of efficiency for FAFs in relation to domestic firms (DFs) in the industry.

When FAFs with their superior *resources and capabilities* interact, transact and compete with DFs for a reasonable period of time in an industry, the latter group may also realize efficiency gains, mainly through two channels: the competition effects and knowledge spillovers[5] generated by demonstration/imitation effects and movement of employees with superior skill set from FAFs to DFs (Smeets 2008). Therefore, the TE may also be positively related to the FAFs penetration in IMI (henceforth FS). Thus, the study tests two hypotheses: (i) FAFs are more efficient than DFs and (ii) TE will be positively related to FS.

Intensity in the import of disembodied technology (IMDT). Arms length import of disembodied technology fills the gap (e.g. the lack of basic or/and detailed designs and drawings capabilities in IMI) in domestically available technology. By using imported disembodied technology, a firm may either introduce a new or improved version of a product in the market or increase efficiency in the use of resources in the plant. In the former cases, the firm's revenue earning capacity may increase; while in the latter case, the firm may save on its resources. Thus, a positive relationship is expected between TE and IMDT.

Capital intensity (CAPI). Being a medium- and high-technology producer goods industry, the goods produced in IMI are required to have high level of precision, performance, finish, quality, etc. Therefore, the efficiency enhancing efforts of a firm may require higher use of information and communication technology, greater automation and frequent modernization of its plant and machinery. Besides, as the opportunity cost of unused plant and machinery could be very high, firms shall be under pressure to use their machinery and equipment efficiently. TE is expected to be positively related to CAPI.

Intensity in the import of intermediate goods (IMIG). The import of intermediate goods, including raw material, capital goods, spare parts and stores, may add to the technological strength of a firm and fulfil the special quality or production requirements of the final goods that cannot be met through the domestically available inputs (in some cases relevant inputs may not be domestically available at all). Therefore, a firm with higher intensity to import intermediate goods may produce output with greater value addition or produce the same output with savings on the resources. Hence, a positive relationship is hypothesized between TE and IMIG.

Export (XD). Export activity makes a firm more efficient on account of knowledge spillovers from its competitors and customers besides its exposure to more competitive (and sometimes advance) international market (Wagner 2007). Global value chains (GVCs) approach emphasizes on the importance of export activity in enhancing the technological capabilities (i.e. learning by exporting) of a firm (Pietrobelli 2007). GVCs are increasingly present in IMI due to the liberalization of national and international regulatory frameworks. Thus, the firms with exports are expected to be more technically efficient than those with no exports.

Research and development intensity (RDI). The most of the existing firms in IMI invest in R&D mainly to develop *in-house technological capabilities* in the form of production engineering, which include operating existing plants and machineries more efficiently; assimilating, absorbing and adapting (to local conditions) the imported embodied and disembodied technologies; and shop floor-based problem-solving related to running, maintenance and repair of plants (CII 2007; EXIM Bank 2008). As most of these activities are efficiency enhancing, the higher R&D expenditures by firms in IMI may lead to higher TE. Therefore, a positive relationship is expected between TE and RDI.

3.3.2 *Other variables*

Advertising and marketing intensity (AMI). Advertising and marketing is used as an important means for creating product differentiation by promoting corporate image, brand equity and customer loyalty. Hence, higher AMI may lead to higher sales, giving efficiency advantage to a firm.

Firm size (SZ). Major factors differentiating a small size firm from a large size firm are the latter's command over a large amount of resources and its diverse capabilities (e.g. risk bearing and innovatory capability), economies of scale and scope in production and bargaining power in accessing financial resources and factors of production from the market. Based on some of these benefits of large size, Hirsch and Adler (1974) suggest a positive relationship between firm size and efficiency. A negative relationship between firm size and efficiency may also exist due to the following reasons: (a) the larger firms are generally afflicted by complex bureaucratic rules causing lack of human relationship and motivation to work, therefore, they may suffer more technical inefficiency than the smaller ones (van den Broeck 1988). Thus, the net outcome of the positive and negative factors associated with the larger size firms shall determine the outcome of the relationship between TE and SZ.

Firm's age (AGE). The firm's age may act as a proxy measure for its maturity, accumulated managerial and other experiences or learning through the execution, operations and maintenance of plants and machinery. Thus, AGE is expected to have a favourable impact on TE. On the contrary, if a firm's age reflects the plant vintage and/or rigidity in outlook or inflexibility towards the changing market conditions, it is expected to have negative influence on TE. Thus, the relationship between AGE and TE cannot be predicted on *a priori* basis.

Networth intensity (NWI): Networth represents a firm's internal and more stable long-term source of finance. Besides, it also gives a firm capacity to raise debt fund from the financial market and institutions.[6] Further, higher portion of networth in a firm's total liability may lead to greater involvement and interest of promoters in the company and enable a firm to undertake expansion or modernization of its plants and risk-taking activities like R&D and exports. Thus, NWI, a ratio of tangible networth to total liability, is expected to positively affect the TE.

Index of market concentration (IMC): Existence of monopoly power or market concentration leads to slack or lack of efforts on the part of managers and workers of a company. Besides, the market leaders in concentrated market structure may prevent entry of superior firms and thereby delay the diffusion of information, technical knowledge and experience sharing. Thus, the industries with concentrated market structure may adversely affect firm-level efficiency. IMI consists of many sub-industries with varying levels of market (sellers) concentration. Based on four-firm concentration ratio of each sub-industries in which a firm operate, a firm-specific IMC is constructed which is expected to affect TE negatively.

Year-specific dummy (YD): TE of the firms are expected to be influenced by year-to-year changes in external factors such as changes in industrial policy, competitive conditions, supply and demand conditions, etc. To account for such factors, the study employs six additive year-

Table 1. Measurement of explanatory variables and expected relationships with TE.

Exp. variable	Definition	Expected relationship with TE
FCD	Foreign Control Dummy (FCD) is a dichotomous additive dummy variable which takes the value 1 for FAFs and 0 for DFs. A firm is defined as a FAF (or DF) if a foreign promoter holds at least 26% (or less than 26%) share in the paid-up capital of the company	Positive
FS	FS is measured by weighted average of FAFs share in gross sales of various sub-industries of IMI in which a firm operates. A weight is calculated as the share of a firm's sales in the sales of a sub-industry in which the firm operate. For computing FS, IMI is categorized into eight sub-industries including: prime movers, engines, boilers and turbines (SI0); fluid power equipment, pumps, compressors, taps and valves (SI1); bearings, gears, gearing and driving elements (SI2); agricultural and forestry machinery (SI3); metal forming machinery and machine tools (SI4); machinery for lifting and handling goods/humans, earthmoving, mining, quarrying, construction (SI5); machinery for food, beverages, tobacco processing, textiles apparel and leather production (SI6) and other industrial machineries (SI7). A minimum 51% of gross sales made up from a sub-industry in a particular FY is used as the norm for this reclassification. The procedure for obtaining FS is illustrated by the following example. Suppose a firm with gross sales of Rs 15 crore operates in two sub-industries of IMI, namely with sales turnover of Rs 10 crore in SI1 and Rs 5 crore in SI2. FAFs' share constitutes 30% in gross sales of SI1 and 15% in the gross sales of SI2. FS is calculated as $0.25 = (10/15)*0.30 + (5/15)*0.15$	Positive
IMDT	Ratio of a firm's expenditure on payments of royalty and technical fees for the import of disembodied technology	Positive
IMIG	Ratio of a firm's combined expenditure on import of raw material, components, spare parts and capital goods to net sales	Positive
CAPI	Ratio of a firm's original cost of plant and machinery to its wage bill	Positive
XD	Dummy variable takes value 1 for exporting firm and 0 for non-exporting ones	Positive
RDI	Ratio of R&D expenditure to net sales	Positive
AMI	Ratio of a firm's expenditure on advertising and marketing to net sales	Positive
SZ	Natural logarithmic value of net sales of a firm in a year. This measure of firm size reduces degree of variability in size across firms and thereby avoids the problem of heteroskedasticity in the estimation of a regression equation	?
AGE	Age of a firm is measured by the difference between its year of presence in the sample and its year of incorporation. As every year of operation may not add significantly to the experience (or plant vintage), natural logarithm of firm's age (AGE) is taken to reduce the variability	?
NWI	Ratio of networth (equity capital plus reserves excluding revaluation reserves) to total liability	Positive
IMC	Sales weighted average of an index of four-firm seller concentration ratio (SCR4) of each of the eight sub-industries of IMI in which a firm operates	Negative

Note: FCD, foreign control dummy.

83

specific dichotomous dummy variables (YD), corresponding to the six years of the study covering the 2001/2002–2006/2007 with reference to the year 2000/2001. Table 1 summarizes the explanatory variables used in the model, their measurements and expected relationship between TE and the explanatory variables.

4. Sample, period and data sources

Empirical analysis in this study employ 940 observations, spread over seven-year period (2000/2001–2006/2007), from a sample of 178 machinery manufacturing firms identified mainly with the help of facilities in PROWESS. The sample includes those firms for which data on each of the variables used for the study are available in PROWESS for at least two years of the study. Besides, the sample excludes sick companies i.e. the companies with non-positive networth in a FY for two reasons: (i) with a view to remove probable outlier effect on the empirical analysis and (ii) the financial statements of sick companies cannot be trusted as many promoters declare their companies sick to obtain the benefits of rehabilitation package, delay the payment of dues to or prevent strong recovery actions from the financial institutions. Thus, the number of sample firms get reduced than that covered in the PROWESS database. Out of the aggregate PROWESS data of IMI on sales turnover, networth, gross fixed assets, total assets, exports and imports, respectively, the sample firms shared 68% of sales turnover, 85% of networth, 74% of gross fixed assets, 69% of total assets, 66% of exports and 74% of imports, where data on each variable are averaged over 2000/2001–2006/2007. Considering the fact that PROWESS covers almost entire corporate sector and 70% of the manufacturing activity, this sample with such shares can be considered as the good representative of the IMI.

The study uses data for the post-1991 reform period of 2000/2001–2006/2007 for two reasons. First, the period of study is more or less stable and marked with the consistent growth in the Indian economy. The study has not included the period after 2006/2007 as the use of longer period could lead to instability in efficiency estimates as well as in the coefficients of their determinants, particularly in view of adverse developments in the world economy including Indian economy due to sub-prime crisis. Second, most of the better accounting standards and practices were introduced after the year 2000, which have, made the financial statements more detailed, transparent, accurate and uniform and thereby comparable across the firms (Mukherjee 2008, Chapter 3). As our study uses firm-level data originally sourced from the annual reports of the companies containing audited financial statements, these developments add additional feature to our study against the studies that have used data pertaining to the period prior to the year 2000.

The study sources major portion of the basic data for designing most of the variables from the annual financial statements of companies as given in PROWESS. The PROWESS, however, provides inadequate data on the foreign promoter's equity participation in a firm. These data were supplemented from other sources (viz. *Bombay Stock Exchange Directory* and *Capital Line Ole* – another electronic database) and *Annual Reports* of some companies. The variable IMC is constructed primarily from the data given in *Industry Market Size and Share* published by the Centre for Monitoring Economy. Data on price deflators for each year of analysis are collected from various publications of the GoI. Relevant product/industry-wise data are used on *Wholesale Price Index* (WPI) (base year 1993–1994) from the WPI series published by the Office of Economic Advisor. Data on wage deflators are sourced from the *All India Consumer Price Index (CPI) Numbers (General) for Industrial Worker* (base year 1982) prepared by the Labour Bureau. With the help of compiled data, appropriate firm-level and sub-industry level indicators are designed.

Table 2 reports the descriptive statistics of individual variables used in the study. Computations on variance inflation factor and tolerance factor, as given in Table 3, reveal no serious

Table 2. Descriptive statistics of variables, 2000/2001–2006/2007.

Variable		Mean	Std. dev.	Min.	Max.
TE	Overall	0.7096	0.0816	0.5377	0.9934
	Between		0.0838	0.5447	0.9932
	Within		0.0028	0.7025	0.7156
FCD	Overall	0.2788	0.4487	0.0000	1.0000
	Between		0.4301	0.0000	1.0000
	Within		0.0000	0.2788	0.2788
FS	Overall	0.2171	0.1219	0.0101	0.4662
	Between		0.1191	0.0136	0.4299
	Within		0.0232	0.1303	0.3261
IMDT	Overall	0.0031	0.0074	0.0000	0.0743
	Between		0.0060	0.0000	0.0372
	Within		0.0040	−0.0215	0.0547
CAPI	Overall	4.7216	5.0334	0.2844	50.0000
	Between		5.0590	0.3259	39.5469
	Within		1.2665	−4.5606	15.1747
IMIG	Overall	0.0930	0.1027	0.0050	0.5823
	Between		0.0918	0.0015	0.4633
	Within		0.0455	−0.1904	0.4421
XD	Overall	0.5684	0.4956	0.0000	1.0000
	Between		0.4262	0.0000	1.0000
	Within		0.2704	−0.2888	1.4255
RDI	Overall	0.0035	0.0060	0.0000	0.0398
	Between		0.0053	0.0000	0.0284
	Within		0.0027	−0.0093	0.0260
AMI	Overall	0.0309	0.0333	0.0000	0.2506
	Between		0.0314	0.0000	0.2197
	Within		0.0127	−0.0548	0.1597
SZ	Overall	3.4278	1.6245	−0.1372	8.8828
	Between		1.5575	0.2772	8.5254
	Within		0.2773	2.1015	4.9944
AGE	Overall	3.1944	0.7298	0.0000	4.6250
	Between		0.7373	0.8959	4.6000
	Within		0.1266	2.0978	3.8896
NWI	Overall	0.4426	0.2034	0.0105	0.9517
	Between		0.1996	0.0304	0..8744
	Within		0.1070	−0.0449	0.6565
IMC	Overall	0.4038	0.1596	0.1256	0.8955
	Between		0.1523	0.1580	0.7762
	Within		0.0568	−0.0171	0.6845

multicolinearity problem in terms of the rule of thumb, as the variance inflation factor for the individual regressors are much below 10.

5. Econometric models and procedure

5.1 *Empirical model for computing TE through SFPF*

To study the determinants of TE, firm- and year-specific TE is required in the first place. To calculate these, the study follows Battese and Coelli's (1992) specification of SFPF model meant for unbalanced panel data with firm effect. For empirical estimation, log linear form of Cobb-Douglas production function is selected for its simplicity.[7]

Table 3. Indicators of multicolinearity: variance inflation factors (VIFs).

Variable	VIF
FS	2.53
YD03	1.80
YD05	1.80
YD02	1.78
YD07	1.77
YD06	1.76
YD04	1.75
SZ	1.64
FCD	1.37
IMIG	1.34
RDI	1.26
IMC	1.25
AGE	1.19
CAPI	1.16
IMDT	1.15
XD	1.14
NWI	1.11
AMI	1.07
Mean VIF	1.42

Accordingly, the model is symbolically presented as follows:

$$\ln Y_{jt} = b_0 + b_1 \ln M_{jt} + b_2 \ln L_{jt} + b_3 \ln K_{jt} + V_{jt} - U_{jt}, \tag{1}$$

$$U_{jt} = \exp\{-\eta(t - T)\} \cdot U_j. \tag{2}$$

The Y, M, L and K represent output, material input, labour input and capital input, respectively. Construction and measurement of these variables are discussed in Appendix 1. The subscript j ($j = 1,\ldots, N$) refers to the jth sample firm (or group); t ($t = 1,\ldots, T$) represents year of operation. The ln symbolizes natural logarithm and b_0, b_1, b_2, b_3 are unknown coefficients to be estimated. The random error component V_{jt} reflect two-side 'statistical noise' which accounts for the effect of such factors as the measurement error, luck, machine performance, etc.; V_{jt} are assumed to be independently and identically distributed (iid) as $N(0, \sigma_v^2)$ and to be independent of U_{jt} and the input vector. U_j are non-negative random variable which ensures that the firm's actual production point lies beneath the stochastic frontier. In other words, U_j are assumed to account for technical inefficiency in production. Statistically, U_j are assumed to be iid as truncations as zero of the $N(\mu, \sigma_u^2)$ distribution. Eta (η) is an unknown scalar parameter to be estimated.

Given the models (1) and (2), Battese and Coelli's (1992) defines operational (minimum mean-squared error) predictor of TE of firm j for the year t (i.e. TE_{jt}) as

$$E[\exp(-U_{jt})|W_j] = \frac{1 - f[\eta_{jt}\sigma_j^* - (\mu_j^*/\sigma_j^*)]}{1 - f(-\mu_j^*/\sigma_j^*)} \exp[-\eta_{jt}\mu_j^* + (1/2)\eta_{jt}^2\sigma_j^{*2}], \tag{3}$$

where W_j ($\equiv V_{jt} - U_j$) represents the ($T_j \times 1$) vector of W_{jt} associated with the time periods observed for the jth firm

$$\mu_j^* = \frac{[\mu \, \sigma_v - \eta_j' W_j \sigma^2]}{[\sigma_v^2 + \eta_j' \eta_j \sigma^2]},$$ (4)

$$\sigma_j^{*2} = \frac{[\sigma_v^2 \sigma^2]}{[\sigma_v^2 + \eta_j' \eta_j \sigma^2]},$$ (5)

where η_j represents the $(T_j \times 1)$ vector of η_{jt} associated with the time periods observed for the jth firm. The function $f(\cdot)$ denotes the probability distribution function for the standard normal variable. The SFPF model, defined by Equations (1) and (2), contains four b-parameters and four additional parameters (σ^2, γ, η and μ) associated with the distributions of the V_{jt} and U_{jt}. The model is estimated by readily available software FRONTIER 4.1 which gives maximum likelihood (ML) estimates of all the parameters of the equations as well as firm- and year-specific TE for every sample firm in the case of unbalanced panel data (Coelli 1996).

5.2 *Empirical model for the determinants of TE*

Following Maddala (1987), the study employs random-effect panel data regression model with Tobit specification for analysing the determinants of TE. Use of Tobit model is necessitated by the fact that the TE estimates lies in the limited range of zero and one. The use of panel data improves the efficiency of econometric estimates on account of larger number of observation compared to the individual data set of cross-section or time series. Besides improving the efficiency, the application of panel data model in this study shall enable us to control for time invariant firm-specific heterogeneity in TE arising from the unobserved firm-specific characteristics. The empirical form of the Tobit model is symbolically represented by the following equation:

$$\begin{aligned}
\text{TE}_{jt} = {} & b_0 + b_1 \, \text{FCD}_{jt} + b_2 \, \text{FS}_{jt} + b_3 \, \text{IMDT}_{jt} + b_4 \, \text{CAPI}_{jt} + b_5 \, \text{IMIG}_{jt} + b_6 \, \text{XD}_{jt} \\
& + b_7 \, \text{RDI}_{jt} + b_8 \, \text{AMI}_{jt} + b_9 \, \text{SZ}_{jt} + b_{10} \, \text{AGE}_{jt} + b_{11} \, \text{NWI}_{jt} + b_{12} \, \text{IMC}_{jt} \\
& + b_{13} \, \text{YD02} + \cdots + b_{18} \, \text{YD07} + u_j + v_{jt},
\end{aligned}$$ (6)

$$j = 1, \ldots, 178 \text{ and } t = 1, \ldots, 7; \quad \text{TE}_{jt} = \text{TE}_{jt}^* \text{ if } \text{TE}_{jt}^* > 0, \ \text{TE}_{jt} = 0 \text{ if } \text{TE}_{jt}^* \leq 0$$

where the term u_j are unobserved stochastic heterogeneity varying across groups but not over time and distributed as $u_j \tilde{I} N(0, \sigma_u^2)$. The error term v_{jt} vary across groups and over times and $v_{it} \tilde{I} N(0, \sigma_v^2)$. The term u_j are assumed to be uncorrelated with v_{jt} and the explanatory variables in Equation (6). The model represented by Equation (6) is estimated by ML estimation technique.

6. Results and discussions

6.1 *SFPF and TE*

Table 4 presents the results of the ML estimates of parameters of SFPF. The results show that the estimates of production function coefficients, signifying elasticity of output with respect to material, labour and capital input, are statistically significant. Elasticity of output with respect to material input (0.71) is the highest and substantial, followed by elasticity of output with respect to labour (0.14) and capital input (0.10), respectively. Although the value of the coefficient associated with material input is substantial, it is much less than the unity which justifies the use of

Table 4. Maximum likelihood estimates of parameters of SFPF.

Variable/parameters	Coefficient	t-Ratio
Ln M	0.71	85.68*
Ln W	0.14	8.13*
Ln C	0.10	6.83*
Constant	1.20	29.17*
Sigma $-$ squared $(\sigma_s^2) \equiv \sigma_v^2 + \sigma^2$	0.03	5.62*
Gama $(\gamma) = \sigma^2/\sigma_s^2$	0.78	32.13*
Mu (μ)	0.31	9.44*
Eta (η)	0.01	0.84
Log likelihood function	705.57	
Lagrange (LR) ratio test of the one-sided error	462.36	
Number of cross-section	178	
Number of years	7	
Number of observations	940	
Number of observations not in the panel	306	

*Shows that the coefficient is significant at 1% level.

three input production functions. Notably, when one uses two input production functions, ignoring raw material, one implicitly assumes that the coefficient associated with material input is close to unity. Further, return to scale, measured as a sum total of these elasticities (0.95), is close to unity, indicating that the production technology is characterized by constant returns to scale.

The analysis of data on the TE_{jt} suggests that: (a) the mean value of TE works out to 71% with higher between variation (0.084) than the within variation (0.003) as measured by standard deviation; (b) group of FAFs with mean TE of 74% is more efficient than the DFs with mean TE of 70%; (c) the most technically efficient firm with mean TE of 99.3% belongs to the group of FAFs, whereas the least technically efficient firm with mean TE of 55.5% belongs to the group of DFs; (d) five most technically efficient firms in the sample includes two FAFs, each one with mean TE of 99% and 97%, and three DFs, each one with mean TE of 96%; and (e) five least efficient firms belong to the group of DFs which include two firms with 58%, one with 56% and two with 55% TE.

6.2 *The determinants of TE*

Table 5 presents the results obtained from the ML estimates of the Equation (6). It shows that Wald χ^2 statistics corresponding to the estimated equation is quite high and significant, suggesting that the equation enjoy significant explanatory power in terms of all the variables used for explaining TE. The following paragraphs discuss the results in respect of individual explanatory variables.

Except export participation, all other technological determinants of TE are found significant and positive. The coefficients of FCD and FS are statistically significant and positive. These results imply that the FAFs on an average are more technically efficient than the DFs and the firms operating in sub-industries with higher presence of FDI are also more efficient, after controlling unobserved firm-specific heterogeneity and other factors. This result is in line the findings of some studies, notably the one comparable study on Indian engineering firms by Goldar, Renganathan, and Banga (2004). The coefficient of IMDT turns out to be significant which is in line with the findings of some Indian studies (Ray 2006). Thus, the firms in IMI are able to purchase foreign disembodied technologies capable of enhancing their efficiency in resource use or even providing value-added items. This result is in line with the finding of

Table 5. Technological determinants of TE (ML estimate of the random-effect panel data Tobit model).

Explanatory variable	Coefficient	Standard error	z-Stat.
FCD	0.023	0.001	15.87*
FS	0.026	0.005	5.78*
IMDT	0.462	0.081	5.72*
CAPI	0.002	0.000	20.53*
IMIG	0.018	0.006	3.17*
XD	0.001	0.001	0.81
RDI	0.402	0.097	4.16*
AMI	0.380	0.018	21.01*
SZ	0.002	0.000	5.7*
AGE	−0.002	0.001	−2.67*
NWI	0.050	0.003	18.23*
IMC	−0.028	0.003	−7.94*
YD02	0.001	0.002	0.57
YD03	0.003	0.002	1.78
YD04	0.005	0.002	2.45*
YD05	0.004	0.002	2.22**
YD06	0.007	0.002	4.01*
YD07	0.010	0.002	5.44*
Constant	0.645	0.004	174.12*
Sigma μ	0.057	0.0004	141.29*
Sigma η	0.014	0.0003	43.04*
Rho	0.941	0.0027	
Log likelihood	2310.03		
Wald χ^2 (18)	2866.8*		
No. of observations	940		
No. of groups	178		

Notes: (1) *, **denote level of significance at 1% and 5%, respectively. (2) Z-value corresponding to the coefficient of each variable presented in the tables is obtained from dividing the value of an estimated coefficient of each independent variable by corresponding heteroskedastic panel corrected standard error.

Goldar, Renganathan, and Banga (2004) for the Indian engineering firms. The result on CAPI indicates that the more capital intensive firms enjoy greater TE. Other Indian studies report the direction of relationship between efficiency and CAPI to be industry-specific.[8] The relationship between TE and IMIG is found significantly positive, implying that the greater use of imported input improves the TE in general. This endorses the findings of Goldar, Renganathan, and Banga (2004) and Ray (2006) who suggests that the import liberalization aimed at providing easy access to imported raw material and capital goods has efficiency enhancing effect. Coefficient of XD is insignificant, indicating exports activity do not offer significant efficiency enhancing benefits to the firms in IMI. This may be because firms in IMI are mostly oriented towards domestic market and consider exporting as the residual activity. The estimated coefficient of RDI turns out to be significant and positive, indicating that the in-house R&D contributes in achieving higher level of efficiency. In other words, R&D efforts aimed at adapting the technology, inputs of production or customization of products are benefiting firms in IMI in producing value-added products and/or in reducing costs. Contrary to this finding, most of the Indian studies report RDI having no impact on firm-level productivity/efficiency.[9]

The results on other than technological variables are mostly on the expected lines. The result on AMI shows that the firms spending more on advertising and marketing as a ratio of sales enjoy greater TE. Thus, the product differentiation advantages created through expenditure on advertising and marketing is helping the firms in realizing higher value for their products. The result pertaining to SZ indicates that the larger size firms are more efficient. Thus, augmenting the scale of operation helps firms in IMI to perform better. AGE of the firm has negative impact on TE, probably indicating the association of age with vintage technology, plant and machinery and inflexible attitude of the employee. The coefficient of NWI indicates that the firms financing their activities through higher proportions of non-interest bearing share holders fund are more technically efficient. In other words, the firms with higher gearings are unable to achieve better efficiency levels. As expected, IMC has negative impact on TE, suggesting competition is good for improving efficiency in IMI. This result is in line with the findings of other studies (viz. Driffield and Kambhampati 2003). The results on the coefficients of YD variables indicate realization of higher efficiency in FY04, FY05, FY06 and FY07 with reference to FY01.

7. Conclusions

Adopting the framework of RBV, this study empirically examined the technological determinants of TE during FY 2000/2001 to FY 2006/2007 in the context of IMI. The most important findings of the study is that technological capability and knowledge base built through alternative channels, such as FDI, import of disembodied technology, research and development, use of more capital intensive techniques of production and import of intermediate goods have efficiency enhancing effects on the firms in IMI. Thus, given the current policy of Indian Government for 100% equity participation through FDI, no restrictions on import of intermediate goods and technology and fiscal concessions on R&D expenditure, the firms desiring to expand their base in this industry (nationally or internationally) must built their efficiency advantage through these channels of technological capability building. To improve their efficiency levels, the companies may also focus on building product differentiation advantage through higher advertising and marketing expenditure, enlargement in their size and financing expansion and other needs through higher use of networth than interest bearing debt. Improving firm-level efficiency with the help of technological and other firm-specific factors brought out by the study would not only help creating internationally competitive IMI capable of withstanding the influx of imports, but also generate higher growth in its domestic production and exports. These in turn may lead to increased share of IMI in global production and exports.

The present study is noteworthy for the following reasons: first, this is the first study for the IMI that has employed the framework of RBV for analysing the technological determinants of firm-level efficiency. Second, as the distribution of TE is truncated above unity, the study estimates more appropriate Tobit model than the linear regression model. Finally, the selection of a single industry has reduced heterogeneity of firms arising out of industry-specific characteristics besides the use of panel data model controls firm-level unobserved heterogeneity (which may arise due to firm-specific product profile, culture, routines, etc.) within the selected industry. However, the limitation of this approach is that the findings of the study may be specific to this industry and thereby cannot be generalized.

Acknowledgements

The author gratefully acknowledges the encouragements and useful comments given by Professor N.S. Siddharthan, MSE, Chennai and Professor B.L. Pandit, Delhi School of Economics, Delhi. The author also thanks two anonymous referees for their comments and suggestions. However, the views expressed in this article are entirely personal and cannot be attributed to the organization (IDBI BANK) in which the author serves or the scholars who have given comments on the article.

Notes

1. DEA – a mathematical programming technique – is an alternative methodology popular among researchers for estimating frontier production function. This method has some advantages over SFPF but cannot take care of statistical noise' arising from factors like machine breakdown, measurement errors, etc. which are generally associated with firm-level data.
2. Refer to Keshari (2010), Table 3.10, p. 65.
3. Ibid., Table 3.6, p. 64.
4. Ibid., Table 3.7, p. 64.
5. Knowledge externalities or spillovers at firm-level is defined as the diffusion of knowledge created by one firm or a group of firms (e.g. FAFs) to the other firm or group of firms (e.g. DFs) without the latter (fully) compensating to the former (Smeets 2008).
6. Indian banks generally follow a benchmark of maximum 3.5:1 for total debt to tangible networth and minimum 1.33 (or 1.25) for current ratio as two key criteria for considering a firm for the financial assistance (Mukherjee 2008, Chapter 6).
7. Researchers (Driffield and Kambhampati 2003) have not reported significant differences in the estimation results obtained either from Cobb-Douglas or an alternative form trans-log specification.
8. For instance, Driffield and Kambhampati (2003) find CAPI to be positively related to TE in the chemicals, metal products and transport equipment industry, but negatively related in the food and beverages and machine tools.
9. Refer to Driffield and Kambhampati (2003) for machine tools industry, Goldar, Renganathan, and Banga (2004) for engineering industry and Ray (2006) for manufacturing sector.

References

Battese, G. E., and T. J. Coelli. 1992. "Frontier Production Functions, Technical Efficiency and Panel Data: With Application to Paddy Farmers in India." *The Journal of Productivity Analysis* 3: 153–169.

Bhandari, A. K., and P. Maiti. 2007. "Efficiency of Indian Manufacturing Firms: Textile Industry as a Case Study." *International Journal of Business and Economics* 6 (1): 71–81.

CII. 2007. *Final Report on Indian Capital Goods Industry.* New Delhi: Confederation of Indian Industry.

Coelli, T. J. 1996. "A Guide to Frontier Version 4.1: A Computer Program for Frontier Production and Cost Function Estimation." CEPA Working Papers, No. 7/96, Department of Econometrics, University of New England, Australia.

Driffield, N., and U. S. Kambhampati. 2003. "Efficiency of Firms in Indian Industry: The Effect of Reforms." *Review of Development Economics* 7 (3): 419–430.

Dunning, J. H. 2000. "The Eclectic Paradigm as an Envelope for Economic and Business Theories of MNE Activity." *International Business Review* 9 (1): 163–190.

EXIM Bank. 2008. "Indian Capital Goods Industry – A Sector Study." Occasional Paper No. 124. Export-Import Bank of India, Mumbai.

Fahy, J., and A. Smithee. 1999. "Strategic Marketing and the Resource Based View of the Firm." *Academy of Marketing Science Review* 19 (10): 1–20.

Faruq, H. A., and D. T. Yi. 2010. "The Determinants of Technical Efficiency of Manufacturing Firms in Ghana." *Global Economy Journal* 10 (3): 1–21.

Goldar, B., V. S. Renganathan, and R. Banga. 2004. "Ownership and Efficiency in Engineering Firms: 1990–91 to 1999–2000." *Economic and Political Weekly*, Review of Industry and Management, January 31, 39 (5): 441–447.

Hirsch, S., and Z. Adler. 1974. "Firm Size and Export Performance." *World Development* 2 (20): 41–46.

Keshari, P. K. 2010. "Comparative Performance of Foreign Controlled and Domestic Firms in the Indian Non-electrical Machinery Industry: A Micro-Level Study." PhD thesis, JNU, New Delhi.

Keshari, P. K. 2012. "Efficiency Spillovers from FDI in the Indian Machinery Industry: A Firm Level Study Using Panel Data model." In *A Compendium of Essays in Applied Econometrics*, edited by T. Tripathy, P. Bhattacharya and M. Aruna, 24–55. Hyderabad: IBS-Hyderabad, IFHE University.

Maddala, G. S. 1987. "Limited Dependent Variable Models Using Panel Data." *The Journal of Human Resources* 22 (3): 307–338.

Mukherjee, D. D. 2008. *Credit Appraisal, Risk Analysis and Decision Making: An Integrated Approach to On and Off Balance Sheet Lending.* Mumbai: Snow White.

Oczkowski, E., and K. Sharma. 2005. "Determinants of Efficiency in Least Developed Countries: Further Evidence from Nepalese Manufacturing Firms." *Journal of Development Studies* 41 (4): 617–630.

Peteraf, M. A., and J. B. Barney. 2003. "Unraveling the Resource-Based Tangle." *Managerial and Decision Economics* 24 (4): 309–323.

Pham, H. T., T. L. Dao, and B. Reilly. 2010. "Technical Efficiency in the Vietnamese Manufacturing Sector." *Journal of International Development* 22: 503–520.

Pietrobelli, C. 2007. "Upgrading, Technological Capabilities and Competitiveness in LDCs: Global Value Chains, Clusters and SMEs." Study prepared for UNCTAD as a Background Paper for the Least Developed Countries Report 2007, UNCTAD, Geneva.

Ray, S. 2006. "The Changing Role of Technological Factors in Explaining Efficiency in Indian Firms." *Journal of Developing Areas* 40 (1): 127–140.

Smeets, R. 2008. "Collecting the Pieces of the FDI Knowledge Spillovers Puzzle." *The World Bank Research Observer* 23 (2): 107–138.

Van den Broeck, J. 1988. "Stochastic Frontier Inefficiency and Firm Size for Selected Industries of the Belgian Manufacturing Sector: Some New Evidence." In *Applications of Modern Production Theory: Efficiency and Productivity*, edited by A. Dogramaci and R. Fare, 59–101. Boston, MA: Kluwer Academic.

Wagner, J. 2007. "Export and Productivity: A Survey of Evidence from Firm Level Data." *The World Economy* 30: 60–82.

Wu, Z. B., G. Yeung, V. Mok, and Z. Han. 2007. "Firm-specific Knowledge and Technical Efficiency of Watch and Clock Manufacturing Firms in China." *International Journal of Production Economics* 107: 317–332.

Appendix 1. Construction of variables used for the estimation of SFPF

Output (Y): WPI deflated value of production (VoP) represents the output (Y) of a firm in our study. To deflate VoP, year-wise data on WPI is used for a firm's major product group. For this purpose, the major product group of each company is matched with the WPI classification, and the matching price series is chosen for the deflation. If the appropriate deflator is not available, the deflator corresponding to the nearest product group is utilized for the purpose. WPI of IMI has been used as deflator in case of a few very diversified companies operating in IMI.

Material inputs (M): As material input (M) constitutes one of the important inputs in production, many Indian studies have been estimating production function with M as an important independent variable (see e.g. Driffield and Kambhampati 2003). To remove the effect of year-to-year change in prices, M is deflated by WPI corresponding to the main product group to which M belonged. For this purpose, M of each company is divided into various categories and matched with the WPI classification and the best available price series is chosen for deflation.

Labour input (L): Following firm-level Indian studies in recent years (Ray 2006), this study approximates L by total wage bill of a firm deflated by the CPI of Industrial Workers. Reason being that the wage bill captures the skill composition of employees at firm-level.

Capital input (K): The study captures K by the historical cost of plant and machinery (or gross fixed stock of capital or plant and machinery as reported in the balance sheet). Thus, the cost of land and building is excluded from the gross fixed assets. The measure used in this study has limitation since K should be ideally be measured by the current replacement cost of the fixed assets of a firm.

Exporting by Indian small and medium enterprises: role of regional technological knowledge, agglomeration and foreign direct investment

Jaya Prakash Pradhan[a] and Keshab Das[b]

[a]Centre for Studies in Economics and Planning, Central University of Gujarat, Gandhinagar, India; [b]Gujarat Institute of Development Research, Gota, Ahmedabad, India

This study analyses regional determinants of export performance of small and medium enterprises (SMEs) in India. The export determinant analysis brings out the significance of certain key physical and economic infrastructure for SMEs, particularly access to roads, ports and loan finance. Local market conditions, namely the size, growth and per capita income of the host states also favourably affect SME export activities. State's stock of technological knowledge also encourages SME exporting. While direct competition with foreign players tends to dampen exporting by SMEs, foreign shareholding participation in SMEs allows affiliated firms to achieve higher level of exports. Apart from improving the key business support infrastructure, export orientation of SMEs could be enhanced by networking them with R&D facilities and providing them easier access to information about overseas markets. Relatively smaller enterprises need greater support as they are disadvantaged by their size.

1. Introduction

The extant research dealing with the determinants of exporting by small and medium enterprises (SMEs) is predominantly focused on enterprise-specific variables like entrepreneurial/managerial competencies, enterprise-level characteristics and their intangible assets and on external factors like characteristics of relevant industry, national markets, business environments and foreign markets (Zou and Stan 1998; Monolova et al. 2002; Obben and Magagula 2003; Majocchi, Bacchiocchi, and Mayrhofer 2005; Tesfom and Lutz 2006; Pradhan and Sahu 2008). However, the roles of regional factors like the stock of technological knowledge, agglomeration and regional distribution of foreign direct investment (FDI) inflows in influencing small business exporting are yet to be included in the literature.

This is contrary to the growing policy and academic recognition that a nation's competitive and innovative advantages in specific segments of global markets can be related to the rise of a few selected local regions within its physical boundary. The industrial districts and 'innovative milieu' approaches refer to geographically defined productive systems where the economic success of these systems lies in fostering local innovation by ease of information flows, facilitating network linkages and supporting social relations (Lawson 1997). The success of Silicon

Valley, for example, is related to the innovative milieu made possible by the creative synergies based on social networks among the Valley's engineers, managers and entrepreneurs and the drive for cooperative technological developments (Castells and Hall 1994). Firms' innovation and competitive success in global markets, irrespective of their size, can be seen to be regionally concentrated (Porter 1998). The geographical proximity allows firms and organizations of a given region to benefit from interactive learning and innovation through the exchange of tacit and explicit knowledge (Asheim and Isaksen 1997, 2002; Cooke 2001). Therefore, localities, cities and regions are increasingly becoming chosen level for studies on technological developments and competitiveness of firms and nations.

With this backdrop, the present study is an attempt to contribute to the existing knowledge on determinants of SME export by exploring how the regional differences in accumulated technological knowledge, FDI inflows and industrial agglomeration influence exporting activities of SMEs from India. The main contention of this study is that regional factors play an important role in SME internationalization (through exporting) even if one controls for the influences of firm- and industry-specific factors.

The next section provides a brief review of the literature and proposes the key hypotheses. Section 3 spells out specifications of the empirical approach and empirical results and inferences are discussed in Section 4. Section 5 concludes the study.

2. Development of the main hypotheses

The literature on industrial districts (Markusen 1996; Sforzi 2002; Beccatini et al. 2003), innovative milieu (Camagni 1995; Maillat 1998) and learning regions (Rutten and Boekema 2007) suggests that regions reflect territorially defined productive systems with a cumulative process of endogenous resource creation, accumulation, diffusion and transfer. The greater the local resource base of a region in terms of the stock of knowledge and information, institutions and skilled labour force, firms embedded in this region are more likely to gain competitive advantages for export expansion.

SMEs are assumed to face greater difficulty in entering export markets because of their resource constraints in capital, information, management expertise, technology and other intangible assets (Acs et al. 1997; Karagozoglu and Lindell 1998; Hollenstein 2005; Pradhan and Sahu 2008). The existence of a higher stock of technological knowledge in the given region is likely to generate technological opportunities and yield intra-temporal knowledge spillovers so as to facilitate in-house R&D efforts of SMEs. This, in turn, may contribute to higher export orientation of SMEs. The R&D-based models of economic growth also support the view that the flow of new knowledge is directly related to the existing stock of knowledge and the number of scientists and engineers engaged in R&D (Romer 1990; Jones 1995; Abdih and Joutz 2006). Thus, SMEs based in regions with greater stock of knowledge are predicted to capture spillover of ideas from the regional stock of existing knowledge and acquire intangible resource capabilities for venturing overseas markets.

Another spatial factor that may be relevant to the analysis of SME exports is agglomeration economies. The tendency of factor inputs and economic activities to get concentrated in spatial clusters has been confirmed by voluminous empirical literature, including on developing economies (Das 2005; Sengenberger 2009). Regions possessing a high degree of spatial concentration of productive units are predicted to have an edge in exporting as spatial agglomeration manifests in localized knowledge flows and spillovers, labour market pooling, input sharing and demand proximity (Muro and Katz 2010). Physical proximity and locally embedded exchanges are critical elements for firms' knowledge creation activities. Regions with strong agglomeration economies can benefit SMEs by ensuring proximity to consumers, productive resources and access to transport and a business-supportive infrastructure. SMEs may also gain export exposure being closer to exporting firms or being part of the same specialized regional suppliers' networks (Damijan and Konings 2011). Koenig (2009) reported that the decision to export by non-exporting firms positively depends on their spatial proximity to the pool of exporters in a region.

The export success of SMEs may also be shaped by the regional distribution of FDI. Foreign firms have played a crucial role in the export performance of a number of developing host countries (UNCTAD 2002). It not only helps these host economies/regions to expand their supply capacities by transfer of tangible and intangible resources, but also ensures that its affiliated firms have direct access to two-thirds of world export markets associated with the activities of transnational corporations (TNCs) (UNCTAD 1999). In addition to the direct exports by TNC affiliates, FDI may boost export activities of domestic firms through its forward and backward linkages in the host region, knowledge-spillovers and pro-competitive effects forcing its domestic counterparts to learn and implement technological and skill up-gradation to compete (Markusen and Venables 1999). In such a scenario, regions hosting relatively large amount of FDI inflows can be expected to have higher export performance than another region not attractive to foreign firms. Sun (2001) found that FDI plays a strongly positive role in the export performance of Chinese provinces in the coastal and central regions while it has an insignificant role for the western region. This merely reflects the fact that FDI has been heavily concentrated in China's coastal provinces, distantly followed by the central region while the western region received only a marginal share.

The foregoing discussions can be summarized into the following three key hypotheses that the study tests:

H1: The size of the stock of technological knowledge assets possessed by the host region interacting with enterprise-level R&D is an important determinant of SME export performance.

H2: Export activities of SMEs increase with the host region's degree of spatial concentration among local firms.

H3: Higher the FDI stock of a region, higher is its SME exporting.

3. Theoretical and empirical framework of analysis

During the last three decades, the internationalization behaviour of SMEs has received increasing academic attention. Empirical studies have used a number of theoretical frameworks in their analysis ranging from the stage theory of internationalization to international trade models based on firm-specific heterogeneity. A brief review of these theories is provided below.

3.1 *The Uppsala model*

This model assumes that firms' internationalization process is fundamentally shaped by the knowledge they derive from experience in current business activities, market-specific learning and network relationships (Johanson and Vahlne 1977, 2009). The deepening of internationalization of a firm occurs along with an evolutionary and sequential process of knowledge accumulation reflecting firm-specific resources and capabilities for engaging in international business. This approach states that a firm incrementally increases its foreign involvements based on relationship-specific knowledge and experiential learning that it acquires gradually about foreign markets.

A domestic firm gets internationalized in a sequential manner starting with irregular and opportunist exports and then moving on to a stage of regular exports through independent agents, next establishing sales subsidiaries for direct exports and finally choosing foreign production. This gradualist theory is very often suggested as a good representation of firms' internationalization behaviour especially for SMEs (Jones 1999). Global market entry with the least risk and lowest investment modes like indirect exports seems sensible for resource constrained SMEs than the choice of greater risk and higher investment modes like sales subsidiaries. Nonetheless, some SMEs from technology-intensive and service sectors may show a strategy of deep internationalization (i.e., direct exporting or outward FDI) within a few years of their existence, which is known as the phenomenon of born global or international entrepreneurship (Westhead et al. 2001; Coviello and Cox 2006).

3.2   *The resource-based view*

This is another theoretical approach used in the analysis of firms' internationalization behaviour. It is argued that firms' internationalization capabilities are critically dependent upon the size of their valuable resources (Rodríguez and Rodríguez 2005; Roxas and Chadee 2011). Continuous acquisition of resources that are useful, unique and difficult to imitate and substitute can only sustain and improve firms' competitiveness and growth (Wernerfelt 1984; Barney 1991, 2001; Newbert 2007). The concept of resources encompasses physical capital and intangible capital covering technological assets, human capital, organizational capital and social capital. Summarizing a firm as a bundle of these resources would imply that inter-firm heterogeneity in such resources is a pertinent explanatory factor for inter-firm variation in the degree of internationalization.

3.3   *Trade models with firm-specific heterogeneity*

International trade models with heterogeneous firms possess implications for understanding SME export decision. This literature brings sunk costs and productivity as determining factors for a firm's decision to enter the foreign market (Roberts and Tybout 1997; Bernard et al. 2003; Melitz 2003). Some critical level of productivity attainment is essential for a firm to start exporting profitably while paying associated sunk cost.[1] This may imply that SMEs with higher productivity are better placed to commit resources required for overcoming the sunk costs in accessing foreign markets and starting export activities.

3.4   *A review of empirical studies on SME exporting*

These different theories of internationalization have motivated an increasing number of empirical studies aimed at the analysis of SME export behaviour. Pope (2002) analysed motivations for exporting for small firms based in California, USA at two levels – firms with 25 or fewer employees and those with more than 25 employees but less than or equal to 200 employees. Results from the analysis of variance suggest that the uniqueness of product and technological advantages are the two motivating factors for firms with a maximum of 25 employees to export. Firms with more than 25 employees are found to export because they believe that they possess a unique product and technological advantage. Moreover, exporting helps them to achieve economies of scale and exploit foreign opportunities.

Yang, Chen, and Chuang (2004) in their study of a sample of Taiwan manufacturing SMEs found that export decisions of these firms are positively determined by their technology (R&D, technology importing and training investment), firm size (over a relevant range), skills of the workforce and labour productivity. Studies on manufacturing SMEs from South Africa show that enterprise export probability is positively affected by size class, age, competition within South Africa, access to borrowed finance, corporate tax, business linkages and access to information (Gumede 2004).

Ottaviano and Martincus (2011) reports that Argentinian SMEs have higher probability of exporting if they have large size (employment), source inputs from abroad, invest in product improvement and possess higher labour productivity. The export participation of UK firms was observed to be greater for older, medium-sized and foreign-owned firms as compared to their younger, small-sized and domestic-owned counterparts (Requena-Silvente 2005). Fernández and Nieto (2005) found that both export probability and intensity were positively associated with age, size, R&D and foreign ownership of Spanish SMEs. Firms' technological activities (product innovation, process innovation and product modification) and size are shown as important determinants of exporting by Vietnamese SMEs (Ngoc et al. 2008). Pradhan and Sahu (2008) found that export performance of Indian SMEs from the pharmaceutical sector improved with firm size, R&D, imports of capital goods and fiscal incentives.

The available literature, essentially, points to firm-specific factors, industry characteristics and export market features as main factors influencing SME exports. However, the role of regional factors is yet to be appreciated and included into the SME export decision. In addition to the predicted roles of regional technological knowledge, agglomeration and inward FDI, a number of other region-specific variables may be affecting SME exporting efforts.

3.5 *Other region-specific factors*

Regional market characteristics may play a significant role in the regional profile of SME exporting. Theoretically, exporting is more profitable from regions that possess large markets because it allows concentration of production with increasing returns and saving on transport costs (Krugman 1991; Fujita, Krugman, and Venables 1999). Regions with large-sized market and/or higher growth are likely to have the advantage of scale and business-friendly policy regime for promoting firms' export activities. While the regional gross state domestic product (SDP) represents the absolute size of the regional market, regional per capita SDP (PSDP) may be used to recognize the importance of the sophistication of regional demand for product varieties. Technological structure of industrial base of regions may be another determining factor for export performance of host SMEs. As technology intensive products typically account for the fastest growing category in the world trade (Lall 2000) and also they generate extensive knowledge spillovers in the host location, regions with greater specialization in technology-driven industrial sectors are likely to have greater involvement in global markets.

Availability of adequate and good quality physical infrastructure like reliable supply of power, transportation system (roads, railways and airways), ports and excellent telecommunication networks (telephone, internet, etc.) may be crucial for firms' performance in global markets. Trade-supporting role of physical infrastructure has been established in a number of empirical studies (WTO 2004; Fugazza 2004; Francois and Manchin 2007). While high export performance of Asian economies has been ascribed to an improved infrastructure triggering a reduction in trade costs (Brooks and Hummels 2009), poor export performance of African countries has been attributed to infrastructure bottlenecks (Freund and Rocha 2010; Mbekeani 2010). Inadequate and inefficient infrastructure and related services tend to inflate costs of both transportation and production which adversely affect the reliability, flexibility and timely delivery of the supply process.

The export success of local firms may very well be related to the extent of accessibility to industrial and trade finance and insurance products in the host region. In most of the emerging economies, inadequate access to finance has been the single most important constraint on firm growth and internationalization (Morris et al. 2001; Mbekeani 2007; Pradhan and Sahu 2008). As regions vary greatly in terms of sufficient availability of finance to firms, inter-regional differences in building financial institutions and supply of credit, these could be important factors explaining regional differences in firms' export behaviour.

3.6 *Empirical model specification*

In view of the theoretical and empirical background as described above, one may consider SME exports behaviour to be determined by heterogeneity in firm-specific resources, sectoral characteristics, policy incentives and regional specificities reflecting regional market characteristics, regional technological knowledge, agglomeration and regional distribution of FDI. The empirical framework chosen for explaining inter-SME patterns of export intensity (EX_{it}) in the present study is provided below:

$$EX_{it} = F[(\text{firm} - \text{specificfactors})_{it}, (\text{sectoral characteristics})_{it}, (\text{policy incentives})_{it},$$
$$(\text{region} - \text{related variables})_{it}] \qquad (A)$$

In the above specification, a number of firm-specific and sector-level factors are included as possible factors influencing SME export activities. These factors are identified based on standard firm-level literature on export behaviour.

3.6.1 *Firm-specific factors*

Firm size (SIZE) has been used as a proxy for the resource base of the firm and has been found to be relevant for export performance of enterprises (Bonaccorsi 1992; Calof 1994; Roberts and Tybout 1997; Bernard and Jensen 1999; Bernard and Wagner 2001; Kumar and Pradhan 2007). A squared term of the firm size ($SIZE^2$) has also been included as this variable is indicated to have a non-linear impact on firms' export activities (Wakelin 1998; Sterlacchini 1999; Roper and Love 2002; Kumar and Pradhan 2007). The age of the firm (AGE) that reflects the effect of firm's accumulated learning and information over the past (Ericson and Pakes 1995; Jovanovic 1982) is expected to affect positively firm's export behaviour.

The firm's ability to acquire, assimilate, modify and create technology has evidently played a crucial role in the export competitiveness (Braunerhjelm 1996; Wakelin 1998; Bleaney and Wakelin 1999; Lefebvre and Lefebvre 2002; Yang, Chen, and Chuang 2004; Fernandez and Nieto 2005; Singh 2006; Anh et al. 2007). The in-house R&D expenses (RDIN), the technological payments made abroad (ETP1) and imports of capital goods (ETP2) are employed as measures of firm-specific technological activities. While the first indicator measures firm's indigenous technological efforts, the last two variables, respectively, represent acquisition of foreign technology in disembodied and embodied forms. *Ceteris paribus*, in-house R&D and embodied technology imports are expected to help the firm achieve higher export activities. However, disembodied technology imports are posited to have an ambiguous effect as technology contracts to developing countries like India come with export prohibition clauses and with other conditionality like 'no reverse engineering' that may inhibit effective technology transfers (UNCTC 1984).

Given the often high marketing entry barriers in the export market, marketing and advertising expenses can provide an essential complement to firms' competitive strength in the world market (Pradhan 2008). Advertising and marketing expenses (ADV) are critical elements of firms' product differentiation advantages that may play a role in promoting domestic firms' decision to internationalize.

Firms' affiliation to domestic business groups (BGA) can foster favourable conditions which encourage them to undertake export activities. Access to the pool of resources and infrastructure represented by the business group and intra-group synergetic interactions in the sharing of information, inputs, skills and technologies is likely to put business group affiliating firms ahead on overseas expansion as compared to stand-alone firms (Pradhan and Singh 2011). Similarly, a firm's ownership links to multinational enterprises (MNEs) may reflect greater export involvement as the affiliated firm get access to capital, technology, information, distribution channels and marketing skills of the MNEs and the global market controlled by them (de La Torre 1971). Affiliation to foreign firms (AFF) could be more important for export-oriented production in technology-intensive and dynamic products in world markets (UNCTAD 2002).

3.6.2 *Industry-related factors*

Industries differ in terms of the extent of technological opportunities, appropriability, cumulativeness of technical competencies and the nature of the knowledge base (Pavitt 1984; Malerba and Orsenigo 1996; Breschi, Malerba, and Orsenigo 2000; Malerba 2005). Therefore, the extent to which firms from a sector could compete internationally may be influenced by the sectoral technological opportunities. Firms are likely to possess higher product quality and efficiency when they come from sectors with higher technological opportunities which may play an important role in promoting their export activities (Barrios, Gorg, and Strobl 2003). Sector-level R&D intensity (RDS), reflecting differences in sectoral technological opportunities, is thus predicted to favour firms' export behaviour.

The relationship between the level of industry concentration (HI) and firms' export performance is apparently ambiguous. While in one situation the strong market power of firms in a highly concentrated industry might provide more incentive to concentrate on domestic market, in another the dominant firms that possess strong intangible and tangible assets might be inspired to look beyond domestic markets (Wu, Fu, and Tang 2010).

3.6.3 *Policy incentives*

The role of government policy measures in strengthening exporting activities of domestic enterprises often has been emphasized in the academic literature (Fitzgerald and Monson 1989; Roy 1993; Pradhan and Sahu 2008). Public policies cover a wide range of incentives like concessional export credit, tax holiday on export income, duty drawbacks, export insurance programmes, etc. These fiscal benefits (FSB) release additional capital complementing a firm's own resources and may reduce the effective costs of its internationalization.

Table 1 lists all the dependent variables included in the empirical framework and provides the measurement of each.

4. Method of estimation and data sources

The dependent variable in the specified export model A is the export intensity, which is a censored variable. In a given industry, exporting is undertaken by a subset of total firms so that the dependent variable becomes bounded from below by zero value with clustering of multiple numbers of observations. When the dependent variable shows extremely censored distribution, the relevant error term is more likely to violate the classical assumptions of normality and homoscedasticity (Sullivan, McGloin, and Piquero 2008). In such a situation, econometric theory suggests that the Tobit maximum likelihood estimates are unreliable for estimating models involving censored dependent variables. The censored quantile regression (CQR) of Powell's (1986) has been proposed as the more robust technique to arrive at consistent estimates when there is heteroscedastic, non-normal and asymmetric errors (Powell 1986; Chay and Powell 2001; Wilhelm 2008). Unlike the traditional Tobit estimator that requires strong parametric assumptions, Powell's (1986) CQR approach manages censoring semi-parametrically based on the quantile function.

Table 1. Description and measurement of variables.

Variables	Symbols	Measurements
Dependent variable		
Firm export intensity	FEX_{it}	Goods and services exports of ith manufacturing firm as a per cent of sales in the year t.
Independent variables		
Firm-specific variables		
Firm age	AGE_{it}	Natural log of the age of ith firm in number of years from the year of its incorporation.
Firm size	$SIZE_{it}$	Natural log of total sales (Rs. Million) of ith firm in tth year.
Firm size squared	$SIZE^2_{it}$	Squared of the natural log of total sales (Rs. Million) of ith firm in tth year.
R&D intensity	$RDIN_{it}$	R&D expenditure (capital+current) as a per cent of total sales of ith firm in tth year.
External technology purchase	$ETP1_{it}$	Expenses in royalties, technical and other professional fees paid abroad by ith firm as a per cent of sales in the year t.
	$ETP2_{it}$	Expenses on imports of capital goods and equipment by ith firm as a per cent of sales in tth year.
Product differentiation	ADV_{it}	Advertising and marketing expenses of ith firm as a per cent of sales in the year t.
Affiliation to foreign firm	AFF_i	Assume 1 if ith firm has affiliation to a foreign firm, 0 otherwise.
Business group affiliation	BGA_i	Assume 1 if ith firm has affiliation to a domestic business group, 0 otherwise.
Industry-specific variables		
Sectoral R&D intensity	RDS_{jt}	R&D expenses (capital+current) of jth industry as a per cent of industry sales in tth year.
Sectoral concentration	HI_{jt}	Natural log of Herfindahl Index of jth industry in tth year based on domestic sales.
Policy variable		
Fiscal benefits	FSB_{it}	Total fiscal benefits related to export activities received by ith firm as a per cent of sales in the year t.
Region-specific variables		
Demand-related factors		
State domestic product (net)	SDP_{kt}	Natural log of gross state domestic product (constant 1999–2000 Indian Rs.) of kth Indian state in year t.
Growth of SDP	$SDPG_{kt}$	Annual percentage change in SDP (constant 1999–2000 Indian Rs.) of kth Indian state in year t.
Per capita SDP	$PSDP_{kt}$	Natural log of per capita SDP (constant 1999–2000 Indian Rs.) of kth Indian state in year t.
Inputs-related factors		
State power availability	$SPWR_{kt}$	Power generated (kWh) per 1,00,000 population of kth Indian state for tth year.
State road infrastructure	$SROD_{kt}$	Total road length (km) per 100 square km area of kth Indian state for tth year.
State port infrastructure	$SPRT_k$	Dummy variable taking value 1 if kth Indian state possesses port facilities, 0 otherwise.
State telecom infrastructure	STI_{kt}	Telephones per 100 population in kth Indian state for tth year.
State finance availability	SFN_{kt}	Credit advances by Scheduled Commercial Banks (Rs. Crore) per 1,00,000 population of kth Indian state for tth year.

(Continued)

Table 1.   Continued.

Variables	Symbols	Measurements
Technology-related factors		
State technological knowledge stock	$STKS_{kt}$	No. of cumulative patent applications from kth Indian state since 1989–1990 per Rs. 1000 billion of its' real gross SDP in year t.
State's technological specialization in manufacturing sector	SSP_{kt}	Net Value Added (NAV) of high-technology manufacturing sectors as a per cent of NAV of total manufacturing sector of kth Indian state in year t.
FDI-related factor		
State inward FDI	$SFDI_{kt}$	Cumulative FDI inflows since 1982–1983 into kth Indian state as a per cent of its gross SDP in year t.
Agglomeration-related factor		
Spatial concentration of firms	$SCON_{kt}$	No. of manufacturing factories per 1000 sq KM of area of kth Indian state in year t.

Notes: (1) High-technology manufacturing sectors include chemicals, pharmaceuticals, electrical and optical equipment, machinery and equipment and transport equipment; (2) 1 crore = 10 million.

Chernozhukov and Hong (2002) recommended a three-step algorithm for estimating the CQR for samples with heavy censoring and high dimensionality. This method contains the following three steps of the estimation procedure:

(i) Estimate a parametric probability model, $p_i = p(X_i^{*'}\beta) + \varepsilon_i$ for the full sample of observations where p_i is an indicator of not-censoring and $X_i^{*'}$ is the desired transformations of the matrix of explanatory variables. After estimating the conditional probabilities of censoring through a logit binary choice model, next select a subset of observations, $S_0(c) = p(X_i^{*'}\beta) > 1 - \theta + c$, for which the conditional quantile function lies above the censoring point. Here, θ is the preferred conditional quantile to keep the subset of observations that are above the censoring point and c is the trimming constant chosen such that the ratio of the size of the selected subsample to the size of the quantile-uncensored subsample is 0.9.

(ii) In the second step, run an ordinary quantile regression to the subsample $S_0(c)$ to arrive at an initial estimator $\hat{\beta}_\theta^0$. This initial estimator is consistent but inefficient. Next, the final subsample of quantile-uncensored observations $S_f = p(X_i^{*'}\beta_\theta^0) > 0$ is selected using the predicted values of the estimated quantile regression.

(iii) In the final step, the Chernozhukov and Hong algorithm fits quantile regression for S_f with bootstrap standard errors based on selected number of replications.

The present study has used the three-step CQR for obtaining reliable estimates for the specified export model. For our initial sample, more than 65% of the firms' observations possess zero export during the study period 1995–2008. This shows that inter-state patterns of firms' export intensity are extremely censored in distribution.

5.   Data source

The present study has drawn upon the SPIESR-GIDR Locational Data-set on Indian Manufacturing Firms (SG-LoDIMF), a multidimensional dataset compiled for the ICSSR (Indian Council of Social Science Research) sponsored research project entitled, *Exploring Regional Patterns of Internationalization of Indian Firms: Learnings for Policy*. It is a unique database that classifies a total of 8486 Indian manufacturing firms, obtained from the Prowess database of the Centre for

Monitoring Indian Economy (CMIE) (2009), by state and union territory based on plant location, product profile (producer of single or multiproducts) and size of production (capacity/actual). As the location information obtained from the Prowess were not comprehensive and there was no consistent information available on the plant location of 1000 odd companies, those data gaps were filled with the information collected through intensive internet searches of company websites, annual reports, consultancy reports, etc. The Prowess database provides company-specific financial variables like sales, exports, R&D, etc.

The sample manufacturing firms covered in the SG-LoDIMF database are estimated to have accounted for about 58% of national manufacturing exports during 1991–2008 (Pradhan and Das 2012). The identification of SMEs is done based on available firm-specific latest year data on cumulative investment in plant and machinery and specified investment ceilings suggested by the Micro, Small and Medium Enterprise Development Act, 2006. Manufacturing firms with the historical value of plant and machinery up to Rs. 100 million are taken as SMEs and those with above Rs. 100 million are designated as large firms.[2] While all the firm-specific and sector-level variables in the SG-LoDIMF are derived mainly from the Prowess Database of the CMIE, information on regional variables is created based on different published sources obtained from government and non-government agencies.

The annual data related to states' real gross state domestic product (GSDP), growth of real GSDP and real per capita GSDP were estimated based on nominal and real series obtained from various *Statements on State Domestic Product* released by the Central Statistical Organiz-ation (CSO). The yearly data on application for patent filed according to state of origin were col-lected from various Annual Reports of the Controller General of Patents, Designs and Trade Marks. Information on net value added for total manufacturing and high-technology industries used in the calculation of state level technological specialization of manufacturing sector came from various reports of *Annual Survey of Industries* (ASI), CSO. High-technology manufacturing segment is defined to include chemicals, pharmaceuticals, electrical and optical equipment, machinery and equipment and transport equipment. The number of manufacturing factories per state is also collected from the ASI.

State-wise FDI stock was estimated by accumulating FDI inflows data since 1982–1983. The FDI inflows data from 1982–1983 to 2003–2004 are on approval terms and from 2004–2005 onwards inflows are on actual basis. FDI data up to 2003–2004 came from foreign collaborations dataset maintained by the Institute of Studies in Industrial Development and from 2004–2005 the information was obtained from *SIA Newsletter* (Annual Issues) of which various years have been used. It should be noted that the data related to the sub-period since 2004–2005 are FDI actual inflows data classified as per the Reserve Bank of India regions.

The state level tele-density data come from the *Compendium of Selected Indicators of Indian Economy (Volume I)* of the CSO (2009). Total road length information was compiled from various issues of *Basic Road Statistics of India*, Ministry of Road Transport and Highways, Government of India. Statistics on gross power generation by states is taken from the *Annual Report on the Working of State Electricity Boards & Electricity Departments* of the Planning Commission (Power and Energy Division) and various General Reviews published by the Central Electricity Authority, Ministry of Power and Government of India. Credit advance by commercial banks by states is sourced from various volumes of *Money and Banking* brought out by the CMIE.

6.   Empirical results and inferences

The specified export model that involves a total of 20 explanatory variables may often suffer from a number of estimation issues. The problem of endogeneity is an important consideration as a number of firm-level independent variables are not strictly exogenous. For instance, a firm's R&D performance may be influenced by its export activities (Pradhan 2011a, 2011b). Similarly, export intensity possesses a favourable feedback with other factors like firm survival (age), size, purchase of foreign technologies and advertising expenses. To minimize any such bias, the study has introduced all the firm-specific variables, except AFF and BGA dummies, in one year lagged form.

Another serious problem is to address the adverse effects of multicollinearity on standard errors of estimates. A high correlation is reported between firm size (SIZE) and its squared term ($SIZE^2$). So to address this problem, the mean centred series has been used in place of SIZE (and $SIZE^2$).

Within the state-specific variables, SPWR, STI, SFN, STKS and SSP are observed to be strongly correlated with other regional factors. Therefore, we ran five auxiliary regressions fitting each of these variables on selected regional factors with which each had a strong correlation (i.e. variables having at least 0.5 magnitude of correlation coefficient) and residuals from these regressions are used in the place of original variables.[3]

The results obtained from the CQR estimation with 500 bootstrap replications for the sample of single-state-based SMEs over the 1995–2008 period have been summarized in Table 2. Regression 1 attempts to cover traditional determinants of exporting that have received extensive attention in the existing literature. It puts exclusive emphasis on firm-specific factors, sectoral level forces and fiscal incentives that may drive SME exporting. Regressions 2 and 3 while formulating export behaviours try to embed regional market-related factors and other spatial variables, addressing the role of space that may prepare SMEs for export activities. All the estimated models showed up with F-values that are statistically different from zero, thus, suggesting that the specified model succeeds well in explaining SMEs' export performance.

6.1 *Regional determinants of SME exports*

The regional market-related variables, SDP_{kt}, $SDPG_{kt}$ and $PSDP_{kt}$, all turn up with positive and statistically significant coefficients. Export-intensive SMEs, therefore, are more concentrated in host states with large and growing local markets. The results clearly indicate the relevance of regional markets in driving SMEs' export activities. As higher per capita income implies a sophisticated and diversified consumer demand, SMEs supplying to a differentiated local market are likely to go global.

$STKS_{kt}$ has a positive coefficient that is different from zero in statistical terms. It would support the hypothesis that the host region's stock of technological knowledge assets plays a significant role in shaping inter-state patterns of SME export intensity. A higher knowledge stock in a host state ensures that SMEs based therein benefit from knowledge spillovers that can expand their operational focus to global markets.

Among infrastructural variables, $SROD_{kt}$ has a positive and significant effect. It suggests that greater road transportation networks are likely to facilitate the depth of SMEs' export activities. Similarly, $SPRT_{kt}$ is seen with a strongly positive sign suggesting that port facilities do have a favourable role in the export success of SMEs. Again SFN_{kt} has a hypothesized positive sign and is statistically different from zero. This may clearly indicate that credit availability is a crucial factor for SMEs' foray into higher exporting. However, the performances of the remaining two variables, namely $SPWR_{kt}$ and STI_{kt}, do not tread the line of our expectation. $SPWR_{kt}$ has a negative but insignificant coefficient to imply that states generating more electricity are not inevitably the home for export-oriented SMEs in India. STI_{kt} also came up with a negative effect that is statistically significant. This may happen if better telecommunication infrastructure available in host states helps firms to boost domestic/national sales over foreign sales.

$SFDI_{kt}$ comes up with a negative sign and falls in the significant zone. The presence of foreign firms in a state, thus, is an important factor influencing negatively SME exporting. As foreign

Table 2. SMEs' export determinants in Indian manufacturing sector.

Independent variables	Coefficients (absolute bootstrap t-statistic)		
	Regression 1	Regression 2	Regression 3
AGE_{it-1}	−0.761622*** (2.92)	−1.548017*** (5.46)	−1.982970*** (5.45)
$SIZE_{it-1}$	1.574598*** (4.76)	1.448048*** (4.71)	2.049861*** (6.23)
$SIZE^2_{it-1}$	0.909890** (2.42)	0.665689** (1.97)	0.447288* (1.67)
$ETP1_{it-1}$	−0.026153 (0.08)	−0.020104 (0.06)	0.744039* (1.84)
$ETP2_{it-1}$	−0.002754 (0.04)	−0.001806 (0.05)	−0.000809 (0.01)
$RDIN_{it-1}$	0.928124 (1.17)	1.043619 (1.43)	1.175418* (1.69)
ADV_{it-1}	−0.032037** (2.09)	−0.031197 (1.33)	−0.035279 (1.44)
AFF_i	1.487807 (1.53)	2.862851*** (3.42)	1.782884* (1.92)
BGA_i	−0.499359 (1.28)	−0.272847 (0.85)	−1.216902*** (3.02)
HI_{jt}	2.399114*** (7.50)	2.228070*** (7.95)	2.569444*** (6.06)
RDS_{jt}	1.568171*** (4.35)	0.835608** (2.32)	0.895415*** (3.27)
FSB_{it-1}	11.719621*** (32.59)	11.432123*** (33.30)	11.341385*** (31.54)
SDP_{kt}		2.541526*** (10.75)	1.412966*** (4.25)
$SDPG_{kt}$		0.071830*** (2.73)	0.075657*** (2.60)
$PSDP_{kt}$		2.555132*** (6.76)	1.589970** (2.12)
$STKS_{kt}$			0.014152*** (4.52)
$SPWR_{kt}$			−0.019552 (1.61)
$SROD_{kt}$			0.002253** (2.20)
$SPRT_{kt}$			3.765888*** (8.25)
STI_{kt}			−0.157951** (2.25)
SFN_{kt}			0.014135*** (4.25)
$SFDI_{kt}$			−0.056757** (2.56)
$SCON_{kt}$			−0.000156 (0.13)
SPL_{kt}			0.059137*** (4.03)
Constant	−8.210975*** (5.08)	−59.774159*** (10.21)	−41.848632*** (5.08)
F-value[a]	138.31	124.08	81.52
Prob $> F$	0.0000	0.0000	0.0000
Observations	13,011	12,527	12,108
No. of exporting firms[b]	1436	1387	1362
No. of total firms[b]	2777	2695	2624
Proportion of exporting firms[b]	51.71	51.47	51.91

Notes: Dependent variable: export intensity. Absolute value of bootstrap t-statistics in parentheses.
[a]Test values are obtained from the independent tests conducted to check if the coefficient of all explanatory variables are simultaneously zero using the testparm command in the STATA.
[b]Number of firms from the final sample obtained in the second step of the Chernozhukov and Hong's (2002) CQR algorithm as described in the text. For exporters, it is the number of firms exporting at least for a year in the study period.
*Significant at 10%.
**Significant at 5%.
***Significant at 1%.

investments in India have been largely domestic market seeking type (Pradhan, Das, and Paul 2011) and contributed merely 3% of total industrial exports from India in 1991 (UNCTAD 2002), SMEs may have been adversely influenced. When the negative competition effects of market seeking FDI overwhelmed its positive knowledge spillover and linkage effects, SMEs are likely to get aggressive on domestic market where they already have a fringe status.

$SCON_{kt}$ turns up with a negative sign but fails to reach the level of statistical significance. Thus, SMEs' export activities are marginally linked to the agglomeration advantages that the spatial concentration of productive units offer to host states. However, the significantly positive coefficient of SPL_{kt} for SMEs indicates that states with technology-intensive production structure are likely to have a competitive SME sector engaged in exports.

6.2 Firm characteristics in SME exports

The coefficient of AGE_{it-1} is significant for SMEs with a negative sign. This shows that SMEs that succeed in exporting are generally young firms. Therefore, newly established SMEs with some critical scale are more export oriented than older SMEs suggesting the phenomenon of 'born global'.

$SIZE_{it-1}$ and $SIZE^2_{it-1}$ both came up with statistically significant positive signs. Hence, a growing size is likely to drive export activities of SMEs at an increasing rate. This suggests that there is no limit for the positive effect of increasing size on export intensity of SMEs.

Of the two variables related to foreign technology imports, $ETP2_{it-1}$ had a negative sign throughout but not significant. $ETP1_{it-1}$ has been found with a positive sign with significance at 10% level for full specification (i.e., regression 3) while it had insignificant negative signs for others. This suggests that the disembodied mode of foreign technology imports is not a relevant source of export advantage for Indian SMEs while embodied forms may be helping them modestly in internationalization capabilities.

$RDIN_{it-1}$ exerts a positive effect on export intensity of SMEs but it is modestly significant for the full specification alone (i.e., regression 3). It would appear, thus, that export advantages of Indian SMEs are derived from factors other than in-house R&D and if there is any role that R&D may have played that is fairly small. It could be due to weak R&D spending by SMEs (Pradhan 2011b) or the predominantly adaptive nature of R&D undertaken by them.

ADV_{it-1} had a strongly negative sign for the specification dealing with firm-specific, sectoral and policy-level factors. For the extended specifications (i.e., regressions 2 and 3) that include regional factors, its effect turns out to be statistically not different from zero. These mixed findings may suggest that SMEs are less likely to be using advertising as a tool of export competitiveness.

Among two ownership-related variables, AFF_i has a predicted positive sign throughout and is significant for extended specifications. Thus, SMEs with foreign shareholders may possess greater export depth than purely domestic owned SMEs. BGA_i consistently came out with a negative sign and assumed significance in the full specification (i.e., regression 3). Therefore, business group affiliated SMEs are likely to have lower export intensity. It could be that BGA while entering the export arena take the scale factor seriously and only affiliated large firms are encouraged to export while affiliated SMEs are inspired to focus more on supplying low-cost components to group-affiliated companies.

6.3 Sectoral determinants of SME exports

HI_{jt} poses a strongly positive effect on export intensity of Indian SMEs. Thus, an increasing concentration in domestic markets may force SMEs with smaller market shares to seek new markets through exports.

RDS_{jt} comes up with a strongly positive coefficient throughout. Thus, R&D intensive industries are likely to be the home for export-intensive SMEs than low-technology industries.

6.4 Fiscal policy and SME exports

FSB_{it-1} has a predicted positive sign throughout and is statistically significant. This would affirm that government fiscal incentives strongly encourage SMEs to export a greater share of their production.

7. Concluding remarks

This study has integrated the role of spatial variables into the analysis of SME export behaviour. The three key hypotheses examined are whether SME exporting improves with the host state's stock of technological knowledge, FDI stock and level of industrial agglomeration. Regional heterogeneity is conceptualized in terms of regional market characteristics, physical infrastructure, technological knowledge stock, agglomeration, technological specialization of production and FDI stock.

Preliminary findings indicate that all the three indicators of local markets, namely, the size, growth and per capita income of the host states favourably affect SME export activities. This implies that for encouraging SME exports smaller and low-income states have to make greater efforts than that by larger states. If their SMEs are overwhelmingly local/regional market dependent, to start with low-income states could actively encourage their firms to achieve national market focus. It might be useful if these state governments extend assistance to their SME entrepreneurs to open distribution centres in other states and participate in fairs and exhibition there.

The results indicate that SMEs export more if host states possess higher stock of technological knowledge.

States' efforts in promoting industrial R&D and innovation, therefore, are very important for greater export performance by their SME sector. Exports by SMEs are found to be further positively influenced by a set of state-specific factors like road length, presence of port facilities, availability of credit and technological specialization of manufacturing production.

Thus, it is important that state governments pay serious attention towards improving and maintaining quality of their roads. Inadequate transportation facilities are likely to erode the competitiveness of SMEs for export activities. In view of the positive role of port facilities in SME exports, a careful look at SMEs' access to port facilities may be required. Coastal states can focus on developing and strengthening port facilities while non-coastal states should plan good quality roads linking their principal manufacturing sites to port facilities in nearby states.

Enhancing the credit facility for SMEs may also help states to realize a greater export contribution from the SME sector. Moreover, states promoting technology-based sectors may realize greater SME exports as knowledge-based sectors generate more value addition and knowledge spillovers to other sectors.

States attracting greater FDI inflows are required to pay specific policy attention to their SMEs and help them to maximize benefits from knowledge spillovers and linkages from foreign firms. This will minimize any adverse effects of competition from FDI and enable SMEs to focus for increasing exporting.

The negative impact of firm age suggests that relatively younger units are more active in exports from the SME sector. Hence, state governments may give special attention to older SMEs with the provision of information on overseas business opportunities and supporting training programmes to promote exporting.

The analysis has also confirmed the positive contribution of firm size in driving SME exports. As SMEs inherently suffer from a lower scale, host states could think of clustering of SMEs as a remedial measure. Spatial proximity enables SMEs to enjoy better infrastructure, testing facilities, joint marketing, etc. The poor role of agglomeration variable in SME exporting may further support priority for promoting clustering of SMEs.

Among technological variables, SMEs are found to be modestly dependent on in-house R&D and foreign technologies for enhancing their exporting. As the long-term competitiveness of their SME sector lies in promoting greater in-house R&D activities and acquisition of new technologies, state governments may consider instituting special incentives for SMEs to start R&D in-house.

Acknowledgements

This study draws upon a part of the research project *Regional Patterns of Internationalization of Indian Firms: Learnings for Policy,* sponsored by the Indian Council of Social Science Research, New Delhi. We deeply appreciate comments and suggestions received from participants at the VII Annual International Conference of the Forum for Global Knowledge Sharing, Pune, India, 30 November–2 December 2012. We are grateful to two anonymous referees and Professor N.S. Siddharthan for their thoughtful comments and suggestions. Thanks are due to Ms Arti Oza for research assistance.

Notes

1. They are costs involved in studying foreign demand and markets, undertaking packaging and product adaptation for foreign consumer preference and market standards and establishing marketing and distribution channels.
2. Taking the exchange rate of Indian rupee vis-à-vis US dollar ($1 = 45.93) on 16 June 2006, the day when this Act got the assent of the President of India, the investment ceiling for SMEs is up to US$ 2.2 million.
3. Auxiliary regressions are: (i) SPWR on PSDP; (ii) SCON on STKS, SROD, STI, SFN and SFDI; (iii) STKS on PSDP, SROD, STI, SFN and SFDI; (iv) STI on PSDP, STKS and SFN and (v) SFN on PSDP, SROD and SFDI.

References

Abdih, Y., and F. Joutz. 2006. "Relating the Knowledge Production Function to Total Factor Productivity: An Endogenous Growth Puzzle." *IMF Staff Papers* 53 (2): 242–271.

Acs, Z. J., R. Morck, J. M. Shaver, and B. Yeung. 1997. "The Internationalization of Small and Medium-Sized Enterprises: A Policy Perspective." *Small Business Economics* 9 (1): 7–20.

Anh, N. N., P. Q. Ngoc, N. D. Chu, and N. D. Nhat. 2007. "Innovation and Export of Vietnam's SME Sector." Paper for UNU-MERIT conference on micro-evidence on innovation in developing economies, May 31–June 1, Maastricht.

Asheim, B. T., and A. Isaksen. 1997. "Location, Agglomeration and Innovation: Towards Regional Innovation Systems in Norway?" *European Planning Studies* 5 (3): 299–330.

Asheim, B., and A. Isaksen. 2002. "Regional Innovation System: The Integration of Local 'Sticky' and Global 'Ubiquitous' Knowledge." *Journal of Technology Transfer* 27 (1): 77–86.

Barney, J. 1991. "Firm Resources and Sustained Competitive Advantage." *Journal of Management* 17 (1): 99–120.

Barney, J. 2001. "Is the Resource-Based 'View' a Useful Perspective for Management Research? Yes." *Academy of Management Review* 26 (1): 41–56.

Barrios, S., H. Gorg, and E. Strobl. 2003. "Explaining Firms' Export Behaviour: R&D, Spillovers and the Destination Market." *Oxford Bulletin of Economics and Statistics* 65 (4): 475–496.

Beccatini, G., M. Bellandi, G. Dei Ottati, and F. Sforzi. 2003. *From Industrial Districts to Local Development: An Itinerary of Research.* Cheltenham: Edward Elgar.

Bernard, A. B., J. Eaton, B. Jensen, and S. Kortum. 2003. "Plants and Productivity in International Trade." *American Economic Review* 93 (4): 1268–1290.

Bernard, A. B., and J. B. Jensen. 1999. "Exceptional Exporter Performance: Cause, Effect, or Both?" *Journal of International Economics* 47 (1): 1–25.

Bernard, A. B., and J. Wagner. 2001. "Export Entry and Exit by German Firms." *WeltwirtschaftlichesArchiv* 137 (1): 105–123.

Bleaney, M., and K. Wakelin. 1999. "Sectoral and Firm-Specific Determinants of Export Performance: Evidence from the United Kingdom." GLM Research Paper No. 99/12. University of Nottingham.

Bonaccorsi, A. 1992. "On the Relationship between Firm Size and Export Intensity." *Journal of International Business Studies* 23 (4): 605–635.

Braunerhjelm, P. 1996. "The Relationship between Firm-specific Intangibles and Exports." *Economic Letters* 53 (2): 213–219.

Breschi, S., F. Malerba, and L. Orsenigo. 2000. "Technological Regimes and Schumpeterian Patterns of Innovation." *Economic Journal* 110 (463): 388–410.

Brooks, D. H., and D. Hummels, eds. 2009. *Infrastructure's Role in Lowering Asia's Trade Costs: Building for Trade.* Cheltenham: Edward Elgar.

Calof, J. L. 1994. "The Relationshipbetween Firm Size and Export Behaviour Revisited." *Journal of International Business Studies* 25 (2): 367–387.

Camagni, R. P. 1995. "The Concept of Innovative Milieu and Its Relevance for Public Policies in European Lagging Regions." *Papers in Regional Science* 74 (4): 317–340.

Castells, M., and P. Hall. 1994. *Technopoles of the World: The Making of Twenty-First-Century Industrial Complexes*. London: Routledge.

Chay, K. Y., and J. L. Powell. 2001. "Semiparametric Censored Regression Models." *Journal of Economic Perspectives* 15 (4): 29–42.

Chernozhukov, V., and H. Hong. 2002. "Three-Step Censored Quantile Regression and Extramarital Affairs." *Journal of American Statistical Association* 97 (459): 872–882.

Cooke, P. 2001. "Regional Innovation Systems, Clusters and the Knowledge Economy." *Industrial and Corporate Change* 10 (4): 945–974.

Coviello, N., and M. Cox. 2006. "The Resource Dynamics of International New Venture Networks." *Journal of International Entrepreneurship* 4 (2–3): 113–132.

Damijan, J. P., and J. Konings. 2011. "Agglomeration Economies, Globalization and Productivity: Firm Level Evidence for Slovenia." VIVES Discussion Paper, No. DP-21. Leuven: KatholiekeUniversiteit Leuven.

Das, K., ed. 2005. *Indian Industrial Clusters*. Aldershot: Ashgate.

Ericson, R., and A. Pakes. 1995. "Markov-Perfect Industry Dynamics: A Framework for Empirical Work." *Review of Economic Studies* 62 (1): 53–82.

Fernandez, Z., and M. J. Nieto. 2005. "Internationalization Strategy of Small and Medium-Sized Family Business: Some Influential Factors." *Family Business Review* 18 (1): 77–89.

Fitzgerald, B., and T. Monson. 1989. "Preferential Credit and Insurance as Means to Promote Exports." *The World Bank Research Observer* 4 (1): 89–114.

Francois, J., and M. Manchin. 2007. "Institutions, Infrastructure, and Trade." IIDE Discussion Paper No. 200704-01. The Netherlands: Institute for International and Development Economics.

Freund, C., and N. Rocha. 2010. "What Constrains Africa's Exports?" Staff Working Paper ERSD No. 2010–07, Economic Research and Statistics Division. Geneva: World Trade Organization.

Fugazza, M. 2004. "Export Performance and Its Determinants: Supply and Demand Constraints." Policy Issues in International Trade and Commodities Study Series No. 26, United Nations Conference on Trade and Development. New York: United Nations.

Fujita, M., P. Krugman, and A. J. Venables. 1999. *The Spatial Economy: Cities, Regions and International Trade*. Cambridge, MA: MIT Press.

Gumede, V. 2004. "Export Propensities and Intensities of Small and Medium Manufacturing Enterprises in South Africa." *Small Business Economics* 22 (5): 379–389.

Hollenstein, H. 2005. "Determinants of International Activities: Are SMEs Different?" *Small Business Economics* 24 (5): 431–450.

Johanson, J., and J. E. Vahlne. 1977. "The Internationalization Process of the Firm: A Model of Knowledge Development and Increasing Foreign Market Commitments." *Journal of International Business Studies* 8 (1): 23–32.

Johanson, J., and J. E. Vahlne. 2009. "The Uppsala internationalization Process Model Revisited: From Liability of Foreignness to Liability of Outsidership." *Journal of International Business Studies* 40 (9): 1411–1431.

Jones, C. 1995. "R&D-Based Models of Economic Growth." *Journal of Political Economy* 103 (4): 759–784.

Jones, M. V. 1999. "The Internationalization of Small High-Technology Firms." *Journal of International Marketing* 7 (4): 15–41.

Jovanovic, B. 1982. "Selection and the Evolution of Industry." *Econometrica* 50 (3): 649–670.

Karagozoglu, N., and M. Lindell. 1998. "Internationalization of Small and Medium-Sized Technology-based Firms: An Exploratory Study." *Journal of Small Business Management* 36 (1): 44–59.

Koenig, P. 2009. "Agglomeration and the Export Decisions of French Firms." *Journal of Urban Economics* 66 (3): 186–195.

Krugman, P. 1991. "Increasing Returns and Economic Geography." *Journal of Political Economy* 99 (3): 483–499.

Kumar, N., and J. P. Pradhan. 2007. "Knowledge-based Exports from India: A Firm-level Analysis of Determinants." In *International Competitiveness & Knowledge-based Industries*, edited by N. Kumar and K. J. Joseph, 53–96. New Delhi: Oxford University Press.

Lall, S. 2000. "The Technological Structure and Performance of Developing Country Manufactured Exports, 1985–98." *Oxford Development Studies* 28 (3): 337–369.

Lawson, C. 1997. "Territorial Clustering and High Technology." Innovation: From Industrial Districts to Innovative Milieux. ESRC Centre for Business Research Working Paper No. 54. Cambridge: University of Cambridge.

Lefebvre, E., and L. A. Lefebvre. 2002. "Innovative Capabilities as Determinants of Export Performance and Behaviour: A Longitudinal Study of Manufacturing SMEs." In *Innovation and Firm Performance: Econometric Explorations of Survey Data*, edited by A. Kleinknecht and P. Mohnen, 281–309. London: Palgrave.

Maillat, D. 1998. "From the Industrial District to the Innovative Milieu: Contribution to an Analysis of Territorialised Productive Organisations." *Recherches Economiques de Louvain* 64 (1): 111–129.

Majocchi, A., E. Bacchiocchi, and U. Mayrhofer. 2005. "Firm Size, Business Experience and Export Intensity in SMEs: A Longitudinal Approach to Complex Relationships." *International Business Review* 14 (6): 719–738.

Malerba, F. 2005. "Sectoral Systems: How and Why Innovation Differ across Sectors." In *The Oxford Handbook of Innovation*, edited by J. Fagerberg, D. Mowery, and R. R. Nelson, 380–407. Oxford: Oxford University Press.

Malerba, F., and L. Orsenigo. 1996. "Schumpeterian Patterns of Innovation are Technology-Specific." *Research Policy* 25 (3): 451–478.

Markusen, A. 1996. "Sticky Places in Slippery Space: A Typology of Industrial Districts." *Economic Geography* 72 (3): 293–313.

Markusen, J. R., and A. J. Venables. 1999. "Foreign Direct Investment as a Catalyst for Industrial Development." *European Economic Review* 43 (2): 335–356.

Mbekeani, K. K. 2007. *The Role of Infrastructure in Determining Export Competitiveness: Framework Paper*. Nairobi: African Economic Research Consortium.

Mbekeani, K. K. 2010. "Infrastructure, Trade Expansion and Regional Integration: Global Experience and Lessons for Africa." *Journal of African Economies* 19 (1): 88–113.

Melitz, M. 2003. "The Impact of Trade on Intra-Industry Reallocations and Aggregate Industry Productivity." *Econometrica* 71 (6): 1695–1725.

Monolova, T. S., C. G. Brush, L. F. Edelman, and P. G. Greene. 2002. "Internationalization of Small Firms: Personal Factors Revisited." *International Small Business Journal* 20 (1): 9–31.

Morris, S., R. Basant, K. Das, K. Ramachandran, and A. Koshy. 2001. *The Growth and Transformation of Small Firms in India*. New Delhi: Oxford University Press.

Muro, M., and B. Katz. 2010. *The New 'Cluster Moment': How Regional Innovation Clusters can Foster the Next Economy* (Brookings Institution Paper). Washington, DC: Metropolitan Policy Program at Brookings.

Newbert, S. 2007. "Empirical Research on the Resource-based View of the Firm: An Assessment and Suggestions for Future Research." *Strategic Management Journal* 28 (2): 121–146.

Ngoc, A. N., N. P. Quang, C. N. Dinh, and N. N. Duc. 2008. "Innovation and Exports in Vietnam's SME Sector." *The European Journal of Development Research* 20 (2): 262–280.

Obben, J., and P. Magagula. 2003. "Firm and Managerial Determinants of the Export Propensity of Small and Medium-Sized Enterprises in Swaziland." *International Small Business Journal* 21 (1): 73–91.

Ottaviano, G., and C. V. Martincus. 2011. "SMEs in Argentina: Who are the Exporters?" *Small Business Economics* 37 (3): 341–361.

Pavitt, K. 1984. "Sectoral Patterns of Innovation: Towards a Taxonomy and a Theory." *Research Policy* 13 (6): 343–373.

Pope, R. A. 2002. "Why Small Firms Export: Another Look." *Journal of Small Business Management* 40 (1): 17–26.

Porter, M. E. 1998. "Clusters and the New Economics of Competition." *Harvard Business Review* 76 (6): 77–90.

Powell, J. L. 1986. "Censored Regression Quantiles." *Journal of Econometrics* 32 (1): 143–155.

Pradhan, J. P. 2008. *Indian Multinationals in the World Economy: Implications for Development*. New Delhi: Bookwell.

Pradhan, J. P. 2011a. "Regional Heterogeneity and Firms' R&D in India." *Innovation and Development* 1 (2): 259–282.

Pradhan, J. P. 2011b. "R&D Strategy of Small and Medium Enterprises in India." *Science, Technology & Society* 16 (3): 373–395.

Pradhan, J. P., and K. Das. 2012. "Regional Origin of Manufacturing Exports: Inter-State Patterns in India." *Journal of Regional Development and Planning* 1 (2): 117–167.

Pradhan, J. P., K. Das, and M. Paul. 2011. "Export-orientation of Foreign Manufacturing Affiliates in India: Factors, Tendencies and Implications." *Eurasian Journal of Business and Economics* 4 (7): 99–127.

Pradhan, J. P., and P. P. Sahu. 2008. *Transnationalization of Indian Pharmaceutical SMEs.* New Delhi: Bookwell Publisher.

Pradhan, J. P., and N. Singh. 2011. "Business Group Affiliation and Location of Indian Firms' Foreign Acquisitions." *Journal of International Commerce, Economics and Policy* 2 (1): 19–41.

Requena-Silvente, F. 2005. "The Decision to Enter and Exit Foreign Markets: Evidence from U.K. SMEs." *Small Business Economics* 25 (3): 237–253.

Roberts, M. J., and J. R. Tybout. 1997. "The Decision to Export in Colombia: An Empirical Model of Entry with Sunk Costs." *American Economic Review* 87 (4): 545–564.

Rodríguez, J. L., and R. M. G. Rodríguez. 2005. "Technology and Export Behaviour: A Resource-Based View Approach." *International Business Review* 14 (5): 539–557.

Romer, P. M. 1990. "Endogenous Technological Change." *Journal of Political Economy* 98 (5): S71–S102.

Roper, S., and J. H. Love. 2002. "Innovation and Export Performance: Evidence form UK and German Manufacturing Plants." *Research Policy* 31 (7): 1087–1102.

Roxas, H. B., and D. Chadee. 2011. "A Resource-Based View of Small Export Firms' Social Capital in a Southeast Asian Country." *Asian Academy of Management Journal* 16 (2): 1–28.

Roy, D. K. 1993. "Impact of Incentives on Export Performance of Bangladesh: A Preliminary Assessment." *Bangladesh Development Studies* 21 (2): 25–44.

Rutten, R. P. J. H., and F. W. M. Boekema, eds. 2007. *The Learning Region: Foundations, State of the Art, Future.* Cheltenham: Edward Elgar.

Sengenberger, W. 2009. "The Scope of Industrial Districts in the Third World." In *The Handbook of Industrial Districts*, edited by G. Becattini, M. Bellandi, and L. De Propris, 630–642. Cheltenham: Edward Elgar.

Sforzi, F. 2002. "The Industrial District and the 'New' Italian Economic Geography." *European Planning Studies* 10 (4): 439–447.

Singh, N. 2006. "R&D, Imports of Technology and Trade Intensities: A Simultaneous Equation Micro-Level Examination." In *India: Industrialization in a Reforming Economy: Essays for K.L. Krishna*, edited by S. Tendulkar, A. Mitra, K. Narayanan, and D. Das, 471–491. New Delhi: Academic Foundation.

Sterlacchini, A. 1999. "Do Innovative Activities Matter to Small Firms in Non-R&D Intensive Industries? An Application to Export Performance." *Research Policy* 28 (8): 819–832.

Sullivan, C. J., J. M. McGloin, and A. R. Piquero. 2008. "Modeling the Deviant Y in Criminology: An Examination of the Assumptions of Censored Normal Regression and Potential Alternatives." *Journal of Quantitative Criminology* 24 (4): 399–421.

Sun, H. 2001. "Foreign Direct Investment and Regional Export Performance in China." *Journal of Regional Science* 41 (2): 317–336.

Tesfom, G., and C. Lutz. 2006. "A Classification of Export Marketing Problems of Small and Medium Sized Manufacturing Firms in Developing Countries." *International Journal of Emerging Markets* 1 (3): 262–281.

de la Torre, J. R. 1971. "Exports of Manufactured Goods from Developing Countries: Marketing Factors and the Role of Foreign Enterprise." *Journal of International Business Studies* 2 (1): 26–39.

UNCTAD. 1999. *World Investment Report 1999: Foreign Direct Investment and the Challenge of Development.* New York: United Nations.

UNCTAD. 2002. *World Investment Report 2002: Transnational Corporations and Export Competitiveness.* New York: United Nations.

UNCTC. 1984. "Costs and Conditions of Technology Transfer through Transnational Corporations." ESCAP/UNCTC Publication Series B No. 3. Bangkok: United Nations.

Wakelin, K. 1998. "Innovation and Export Behaviour at Firm Level." *Research Policy* 26 (7–8): 829–841.

Wernerfelt, B. 1984. "A Resource-based View of the Firm." *Strategic Management Journal* 5 (2): 171–180.

Westhead, P., M. Wright, D. Ucbasaran, and F. Martin. 2001. "International Market Selection Strategies of Manufacturing and Services Firms." *Entrepreneurship and Regional Development* 13 (1): 17–46.

Wilhelm, M. O. 2008. "Practical Considerations for Choosing Between Tobit and SCLS or CLAD Estimators for Censored Regression Models with an Application to Charitable Giving." *Oxford Bulletin of Economics and Statistics* 70 (4): 559–582.

WTO. 2004. *World Trade Report 2004: Exploring the Linkage between the Domestic Policy Environment and International Trade.* Geneva: World Trade Organization.

Wu, Y., D. Fu, and Y. Tang. 2010. "The Effects of Ownership Structure and Industry Characteristics on Export Performance: Evidence from Chinese Manufacturing Firms." Economics Discussion Paper No. 10–09, Department of Economics. Crawley: The University of Western Australia.

Yang, C. H., J. R. Chen, and W. B. Chuang. 2004. "Technology and Export Decision." *Small Business Economics* 22 (5): 349–364.

Zou, S., and S. Stan. 1998. "The Determinants of Export Performance: A Review of the Empirical Literature between 1987 and 1997." *International Marketing Review* 15 (5): 333–356.

Index

For Product Safety Concerns and Information please contact our EU
representative GPSR@taylorandfrancis.com Taylor & Francis Verlag GmbH,
Kaufingerstraße 24, 80331 München, Germany

Printed and bound by CPI Group (UK) Ltd, Croydon, CR0 4YY
08/05/2025
01864323-0001